REMINISCENCES AND REFLECTIONS

REMINISCENCES AND REFLECTIONS

Lt. Gen. S.K. Sinha (Rtd.) PVSM

GYAN

Reminiscences and Reflections

Rs. 650

ISBN: 978-81-212-1093-5

Published in 2011 in India by
Gyan Publishing House
23, Main Ansari Road, Darya Ganj,
New Delhi-110002
Phones : 23282060, 23261060
Fax : 011-23285914
E-mail: books@gyanbooks.com
Website: www.gyanbooks.com

Leser Type Setting by : Square Vision, New Delhi

Printed at : Chawla Offset Press, New Delhi

CONTENTS

PART-III
TERRORISM

PART-IV
MISCELLANY

INTRODUCTION

After well over six decades of service to the Nation in various capacities, as a military officer for forty years, as a diplomat for a while and as a Governor for eleven years, interacting with civil administration at the apex level, I felt I had fully earned my retirement in 2008. I looked forward to a life of leisure with no responibilities. My last ten days as Governor in Jammu and Kashmir saw an unfortunate communal storm-based on total falsehood-brewing in the Valley. After my departure from Kashmir, it soon erupted as a communal tornado engulfing the Valley, I found "secular" opinion at the national level grossly misled. A senior journalist in a leading national newspaper and some civil and human rights activists with bleeding hearts, began advocating that India should pull out from Kashmir! I felt it was my bounden duty to dispel all the false propaganda and misinformation that had been unleashed, so that the tragic developments in Kashmir could be seen in their right perspective. Our politicians were too busy preparing for the coming national election of 2009 to give much attention to the fire burning in Jammu and Kashmir. I launched a one man crusade, speaking to various print and electronic media and going on a lecture tour all over the country. I do not know to what extent my humble effort had any impact but I certainly had the satisfaction of having done my little bit for my country. The right epitaph to the three months summer madness in Kashmir of 2008 was the statement of Maulana Mahmood Madani MP. "Transferring of land from the Forest Department to the Board did not hurt Muslim interests in any way. There was nothing to oppose. It was unnecessarily made into a political issue by all sides". The State Assembly elections of late 2008 and Parliamentary elections of mid 2009 vindicated India's stand in Kashmir. Despite the boycott call of separatists and the threat of terrorist violence, the voter turn out was unprecedented. The voter turn out in Kashmir was higher than the national average. Having appeared to have lost the battle for Kashmiriyat (amity across religious divide) we seemed to have got back on course to win the war for Kashmiriyat. That later events and belied that hopk is of course a different matter governance deficit.

Living in retirement, I realized that I now belonged to a vanishing generation, with most of my contemporaries no more. When I interact with the younger generations, they show interest in my experience of the old days and anecdotes about the great personalities of the previous generations. I get reminded of what the then US Ambassador to India, Robert Blackwill, once wrote to me. He had visited me in Assam a couple of times and I had long discussions with him on Assam and also Kashmir. We also discussed some events of the Second World War and of the time when India became independent. On return to Delhi he wrote me a warm letter of thanks. An extract from his letter is worth quoting "It was a profound pleasure to visit the Raj Bhavan and to share some of your remarkable experiences. One of our great statesmen, Dean Acheson coined a phrase which has bcome part of our history - present at the time of creation (referring to the post war international system) - which I think you may quite rightly claim for yourself in the Indian context". At the request of some of my editor friends, I began writing edit page articles in national dailies on my reminiscences and also reflections on some current problems that we face as a Nation. I have been doing this on a regular basis for The Asian Age. Gyan Publishing House, suggested to me that my articles should be compiled in a book so that they are readily available in the future. He added that he will be happy to publish such a compilation. I readily agreed. These articles have been edited and updated. They have been grouped subject wise in different chapters of this book. In all humility, I now present this book Reminiscences and Reflections, to my readers.

PART-I
MEMORIES

1

WHEN BAPU DIED

The Partition holocaust in which millions were killed and millions were uprooted, began on 16 August 1946 with Jinnah's Direct Action Day. It ended with Bapu's martyrdom on 30 January 1948. Unprecedented communal violence engulfed the country in a chain of violence and counter violence.

I served in the Military Operations Directorate at Army Headquarters in Delhi, dealing with internal security from September 1946 to September 1947. In September 1947 I was posted as operatons staff officer to the newly raised Headquarters Delhi and East Punjab Command. In 1948 our headquarters was redesignated as Western Command. Initially we functioned as a self-contained mobile headquarters in a railway train travelling between Delhi and Lahore. Mountbatten had made the Viceroy's special available to our headquarters. This gave me a good first hand view of the tragedy of Partition holocaust.

By January 1948 the situation in Delhi and Punjab had improved considerably. The Army had returned to barracks and was no longer deployed for internal security in Delhi or Punjab. Our Headqurters was now located in the hutments near South Block, where the Sena Bhavan now stands. On 20 January 1948 Lt Gen KM Cariappa took over as our Army Commander from Lt Gen Sir Dudley Russell. I continued as operations staff officer in the headquarters. Our Headquarters which had started as a skeleton headquarters of about twelve officers, all British except me, had now become fully Indian.

We had been given the additional responsibility of conducting operations in Jammu and Kashmir against Pakistan.

I had accompanied Cariappa during a three days hectic tour of Kashmir and returned to Delhi on the morning of 30 January 1948, As I was leaving my office on 30 January a little after 5, my office runner came rushing to me and said that the Mahatma had been assassinated. I was stunned. I had never met the Mahatma. However, as a student I had seen him from a distance in Patna, a part of large crowd at a prayer meeting. It was an unforgettable moment. Everyone appeared overwhelmed with a feeling of reverence for the little man in loin cloth. I had read his biography, Out of Dust, written by DF Karaka in the early Thirties. I was much impressed by that book which had become my bible during my student days.

Within minutes of my getting the horrific news of the Mahatma's assassination, Cariappa came to the Operations Room and asked me to send an alert to all Army units in Delhi and Punjab. Although the radio started announcing immediately that the assassin was a Hindu, we did not want to take any chance. In case the assassin ware a Muslim, there could be a blood bath in the country. We worked all night to deploy troops all over Delhi and alert troops in Punjab. We were given the responsibility to maintain law and order in Delhi while Army Headquarters made arrangements for the funeral. I returned early morning to my father's house on Dupleix (now Kamraj) Road, where I was living. My grandparents were also there. My father was in the Intelligence Bureau and had gone to Birla House where Bapu's body lay and from where the funeral procession was to start. He had to accompany the funeral procession on foot as no vehicle other than the cortege was to be in the procession. My grand parents and my mother wanted to have a "Darshan" of Bapu. Huge crowds were gathering at Birla House and the roads near that place. It was not possible to take them there. It was still early in the morning. I managed with some difficulty to take them to the two storied married army officers hostel on (now Maulana Azad Road). A friend of mine was living there. That building was later demolished and Nirman Bhavan has come up at that site. We managed to go to my friend's flat and from the terrace got a clear view of the funeral procession passing down the Queensway (now

Janpath). We saw Bapu's body on a platform mounted on a truck with Nehru and Patel sitting near his feet. That view has remained clearly etched in my mind.

We returned to our house and as I entered, the telephone rang. The Secretary to the Chief Minister of Bihar was on the line. He was desperately trying to get through to my father to arrange transport to pick up the Chief Minister and two Ministers from the airport. They were coming by a special plane and were due to land in less than an hour. There were no staff cars in those days nor were there any State Bhavans in Delhi. I had no alternative but proceed immediately in my father's car to Willingdon, now Safdarganj airport. Wading through large crowds on the roads everywhere, I managed to reach the airport in time to receive the Ministers. They insisted that I took them to the cremation site. It was a very tall order. I told them that I would do my best but I was not sure whether I would succeed. I drove the car cross country along the Jamuna, East of Purana Qila towards Raj Ghat. I knew that area. It had been the concentration camp for lakhs of Muslim refugees. The Army was deployed to guard the camp and to escort them by train to Pakistan. We had made improvised dirt tracks for vehicles. Some of these still existed. I had visited the camp a few times. I had to do some hard cross country driving through that area for two hours through milling crowds. We reached some 400 yards short of the funeral pyre, which had already been lit. The Ministers got out and went towards the pyre. I stood up on the mudguard of our sturdy Ford and saw the flames from the pyre shooting up. I also saw Mountbatten in his Admiral's regalia sitting cross legged on the ground with Nehru, Azad sitting close to him. They had left their cars nearly a mile away and had walked to the site. After a while the Bihar Ministers returned. Simultaneously, Rajagopalachari, then Governor of West Bengal came. His Military Secretary told me that his car was far away and it was difficult to take him there through the crowd. He requested me to take Rajaji in my car and drop him in Connaught Place, where he was staying. I readily agreed. I again drove cross country for over an hour. The crowd was now dispersing. When they saw Rajaji in the car, they would shout "Rajaji ki Jay." Rajaji would get angry and say that the greatest man in the world had been killed and it was absurd to raise any slogan in his honour. It was fast getting dark. I drove to Darbhanga House on Man Singh Road where I dropped the Bihar Ministers. This building now houses the offices of the Intelligence Bureau. I then drove to Connaught Place where Rajaji was staying with his son-in-law Devdas Gandhi who was the Editor of Hindustan Times. Rajaji insisted that I stayed back and had some coffee. A hot cup of coffee and biscuits were most welcome. Having been up all night and done some hard driving all day without any food, I was dead tired and very famished.

A year later, Rajaji was the Governor General and Cariappa had taken over as the Chief of the Army. Cariappa invited Rajaji for a reception at his house, 4 King George Avenue, now Rajaji Marg. I was also at that Reception and was introduced to Rajaji. He surprised me and others saying, "Of course. I know this young officer. He saved my life on the day of Gandhiji's funeral". I never met Rajaji again.

Every year the Nation pays tribute to the memory of Bapu at a formal function at 11 A.M. on 30 January. The time chosen coincides with the time when the armistice was signed after the First World War. During British days, all traffic on roads used to stop for two minutes. Why don't we pay our tribute to the Father of the Nation at five past five in the afternoon when he died with He Ram on his lips? A siren should be sounded at that time in all cities of India and, all traffic on roads brought to a halt and people stand in silence for two minutes.

2

REMEMBERING THE SARDAR

31 October is the birthday of Sardar Patel. The Nation should observe it as the National Integration Day. His contribution in integrating the Nation will remain unparalleled in history. I had seen the Sardar from a distance a few times. The closest I got to him was when I would see him out for his morning stroll in Lodi Gardens in 1947 accompanied by a dozen or so of his followers. I used to jog in the gardens and when I used to approach him, I would stop and fold my hands in Pranam. He would nod in reply. After a few times, he started giving me a smile of recognition. I fancy that the days when he did not see me jogging, he may have missed me, although he could not have known who I was.

I had occasion to see the Sardar in action from a distance. In 1948, I was a Major serving on the staff of Lt Gen KM Cariappa who was then the Army Commander in the West. I had accompanied the General on a tour to Kashmir in August 1948. We were at Uri one afternoon when we received a message that the Deputy Prime Minister wanted to meet him urgently. Cariappa cancelled his engagements. We rushed back to Srinagar to catch the Air Force plane waiting to take us to Delhi. We drove from the airport to the Sardar's house on 1 Aurangzeb Road. While I waited on the verandah outside, Cariappa went inside. Within five minutes he came back and we drove to his house on Rajaji Marg. In the car Cariappa said, "Rather strange, the Sardar asked me a question and I gave him a one word reply. He thanked me and that was the end of our meeting". Later I learnt what it was all about, some from the General himself during his relaxed moments and some from other contemporary sources.

Hyderabad was the largest Princely State of India. It was of the size of France but was landlocked. The Nizam was toying with the idea of declaring independence. He was then the richest man of world. There were rumours that he was negotiating to buy Goa from the Portugese to find an outlet to the sea. Jinnah wanted Hyderabad to accede to Pakistan. The Nizam got Sir William Monckton, leading lawyer of Britain to negotiate for him with Government of India. Endless talks were taking place for nearly a year. Qasim Rizvi, a Muslim zealot had organized the Razakar party with nearly one lakh members. He also had a youth brigade armed with an assortment of weapons. The Razakars looked upon Hyderabad-Delhi differences as a Hindu-Muslim conflict. Jinnah had threatened retaliation, if India acted against the Nizam. There were reports of gun running by British mercenaries, bringing weapons by air from Pakistan and some European countries. The Razakars were not only committing atrocities on the Hindus, leading to their exodus from Hydearabad, but had got emboldened to raid villages across the border. The Sardar was not the man to take this lying down. He decided that the time for action had come. Jawaharlal Nehru was on a tour out of the country and the Sardar was holding the fort in Delhi. Referring to Hyderabad, Coupland a senior British civil servant had said, "India will live if Muslim limbs in the West and the East were amputated but it could not live without its midriff". The Sardar maintained that Hyderabad was a cancer in stomach of India. The cancer had to be cured if India was to survive.

All the inputs provided to Sardar urged no military action in Hyderabad. The Arny Chief, General Sir Roy Bucher advised that the Indian Army should not be asked to open a second front in Hyderabad when it was embroiled in Kashmir. The intelligence input was that Hyderabad had the largest and most efficient State Army of about 30,000 soldiers with some tanks and artillery. General El Adroos, Turkish Chief of the Hyderabad Army was an able General. Razakars would support the Hyderabad Army. If we invaded Hyderabad we would get bogged down in a long drawn war. We had been through a communal blood bath during Partition. Peace had been restored after a long spell of communal violence. The invasion of Hyderabad may result in another communal flare up in the country. The Foreign Ministry felt that not only Pakistan and the Islamic world but also the West would be against India, if she acted and invaded Hyderabad. The Sardar sent for the two Indain Army Commanders, Rajendrasinghji in the South and Cariappa in the West. Rajendrasinghji assured him that the Hyderabad Army could be defeated in a swift military action. Cariappa was asked if he could defend the Western front against Pakistan without asking for any reinforcements. Cariappa replied in the affirmative. That explained why Cariappa had spent less five minutes with the Sardar. Sardar's mind was made up. He ordered military action in Hyderabad. Within a week the Nizam signed the Instrument of Accession.

Not only in the case of Hyderabad but also on other issues, the Sardar displayed great foresight and remarkable ability to take hard decisions. Having opposed the two nation theory and any division of India all his life, he was pragmatic enough to realize that in the conditions prevailing in mid 1947, there was no alternative to Partition. His decision to salvage the wreck of 1947 was an act of great statesmanship. Had there been any patchwork unity solution with a weak Centre, India may have suffered disastrously. It may not have been possible to integrate all the Princely States. The minority population in India was 12% in 1947. In an undivided India today, it would have been over 40%. Petrol funded Islamists would have swamped the country. India would have broken up into several countries like erstwhile Yugoslavia or would have become a modern Lebanon on a bigger scale. Another instance of his foresight was the letter dying Sardar wrote to Nehru in 1950 warning him about China. Had his warning been heeded, the Nation would not have suffered the humiliation of 1962.

No memorial other than his statue on the Parliament Street has been put up to the Sardar in Delhi, where memorials abound with residential buildings converted for that purpose. I have visited memorial of the Sardar in Karamsad, his village home. It is in the modest double storey house, built by his father, Jhaverbhai Patel. He had fought in the Great Uprising of 1857. He served in the army of Rani of Jhansi. He was wounded at

Gwalior when the Rani attained martyrdom. He was taken a prisoner and released after a few years. On return to his village he had built the house in which his two sons Vitthalbhai and Vallabhbhai were born. No other family in India can boast of such a distinguished record from 1857 to 1947. The room in which the Sardar was born has an eternal burning lamp. Wick and oil for the iron lamp are provided by village panchayat. Hundreds of photographs of Sardar at various stages of his life adorn walls in the house. I enquired if the Sardar, once a leading Barrister at Ahmedabad, owned a house elsewhere. I was told that the house built by his father was his only immovable property. Fabulously rich Princes including the richest men in the world, had knuckled under him. Yet when he died he had a bank balance of Rs 270 only.

Disregarding the near unanimous recommendation of all the Provincial Congress Committees, Mahatma chose Nehru to be the Prime Minister. As a disciplined disciple, Sardar readily accepted the unfair decision. Had the Sardar been made Prime Minister, the history of India may have been different today. Successive Governments of his own party have tried to ignore the Sardar. Not only no suitable memorial was put up for him in Delhi, he was not even awarded the Bharat Ratna for a long time. Fifty years after his death, he was posthumously awarded the Bharat Ratna by a non-Congress Government. Our Government Controlled Doordarshan, known to be His Masters Voice, displays pictures every day of some dozen great Indians, starting from the Mahatma, members of Nehru dynasty and others who contributed towards making India great. Sardar Patel is not included in this list. Let the people of India pay a tribute to the greatest Sardar in their hearts and observe 31 October as our National Integration Day.

3

JP AND 25 JUNE

On 25 June 1975 I was serving as Director Military Intelligence at Army Headquarters in Delhi. I was taken completely unawares when I heard that Emergency had been declared. I started getting daily reports from Intelligence Bureau of situation in the country and the arrests running into thousands being made every day. We recovered pamphlets surreptitiously circulated comparing Hitler's declaration of Emergency in 1933 with the Emergency then clamped on India. The German Army being apolitical had kept itself aloof. Had it intervened, Hitler could have been prevented from becoming a Dictator and the liberal constitution of Weimar Republic could have been saved. There may not have been any holocaust in Germany and mankind may have been spared the horror of the Second World War. I had to monitor reactions within the Army. I found that the pamphlet had no impact and the Army remained steadfast to its apolitical culture.

At the personal level, I felt disturbed by the arrest of JP. My father and he had been students together in Patna and my grandfather had known him from those days. In 1942 JP had escaped from Hazaribagh Central Jail scaling its high wall with the help of several dhotis tied together. I was then a student and JP had become our hero. One evening I went to the house of my father's cousin who was a few years older than me. I was surprised to accidentally meet JP at his house. He was in hiding, with the Police on the look out for him. The following day JP and my uncle disappeared and went underground. They moved to the foothills in Nepal. JP organized widespread destruction of communication facilities both rail and telegraph to paralyse the British Government. On release from jail, Mahatma Gandhi hailed JP as the hero of Quit India movement. After Independence, JP left politics and joined Acharya Vinoba Bhave. Nehru invited JP to join his cabinet as Deputy Prime Minister after the death of Sardar Patel. This would have ensured his becoming Prime Minister after Nehru, but he declined. Similarly he declined to be President of India in late Sixties. During Bihar famine of 1965, JP set up the Bihar Relief Committee to provide succour to the people in famine hit areas. My father living in retirement was invited by him to become the Honorary Director of this Committee. Because of JP's name, funds poured in from abroad and also from Government of India. Hundreds of deep tube wells were dug and hundreds of free kitchens were run. After JP's death my father succeeded him as President of the Committee. In May 1974, I happened to travel in the same flight with JP. To my pleasant surprise, I found JP sitting next to me. That was the time when differences had erupted between him and Indira Gandhi. JP was leading the students' movement in Bihar, which had spread all over the country. We did not discuss a word of politics on the flight. JP was amused to learn that I was then the head of Military Intelligence. On reaching Delhi, JP held his brief case to deplane. I offered to carry his brief case. He said that I was now a General and Generals do not carry a brief case. I replied that I was also a nephew. What would people say if I allowed my old uncle to carry his brief case. He smiled and handed over his brief case to me. A large crowd was waiting for him outside. I handed over his brief case to one of his aides. I saluted JP and departed. Next morning I was with General Raina, the Army Chief, in his office. Raina smilingly remarked that I appeared to be close to JP. I immediately guessed that Intelligence Bureau must have sent a report on me. I told Raina of my old association with JP. He told me not to worry. A few weeks later on 25 June when Emergency was declared, JP was arrested on that date and kept in confinement at Chandigarh. Later he was sent to a hospital in Mumbai for treatment. I used to give intelligence briefing to the three Service Chiefs every week. I mentioned about JP's illness. The Air Chief interrupted asking me, "Hasn't that old man died yet" I looked at him and in a firm voice replied, "Sir, thank God, the greatest living Indian is alive". Raina was the Chairman of the Chiefs of Staff Committee. He changed the topic. Exaggerated versions of this exchange spread in South Block where people had begun to talk in whispers those days. Shortly after, I was posted to command a division in Kashmir. Raina told me that he was sending me to command a division again in the interest of my career before I picked up the rank of Lt Gen. Notwithstanding this, the general feeling was that I was moved out for political reasons. Kuldip Nayyar's book on Emergency: Judgment, refers pointedly to Kaul replacing me. In 1983 I was the senior Army Commander and was brought in as Vice Chief to Delhi. I was told that I would be taking over as Chief shortly. Suddenly, Indira Gandhi decided to supersede me. This caused controversy in the Press and in Parliament. Newspapers reported that I had been superseded on account of my JP connection. I decided to quit the Army and return to my home in Patna.

As I landed at Patna airport I was surprised to find a large crowd led by Karpoori Thakur to welcome me. He was the Leader of Opposition and former Chief Minister of Bihar. There was resentment in Bihar at my supersession on account of my JP connection. I became friendly with Karpoori Thakur. He would often come to my house. I proposed that we should have a bronze statue of JP in Patna without seeking Government funds. He liked the idea and suggested that a committee be formed with me as its President and he along with leaders of the State BJP and State Janta party as Vice Presidents. I said that he should be the President and I could be the Vice President but he would not agree. We met Bindeshwari Dubey, the then Chief Minister of Bihar. He was an admirer of JP and readily agreed to allocate a prime location near Gandhi Maidan in Patna. I undertook a lecture tour all over the country. I received generous contributions and was was able to raise ten lakhs.. We started work on the statue in right earnest and completed the task in record time. The Chief Minister asked me to invite Rajiv Gandhi to unveil the statue. I told him that I had already invited President Zail Singh and he had accepted my invitation. That was the time when acute differences had arisen between Zail Singh and Rajiv Gandhi. The Chief Minister did not want Zail Singh to visit Bihar. Zail Singh's tenure was to end soon. Bihar Government started playing delaying tactics. It intimated the President's Secretariat that the statue was not ready and also expressed reservations about the President's security. I met the President and told him that the statue was ready. I showed him its photograph. I also told him that in case Bihar Government had problems in arranging his security, he as Supreme Commander could get the Army to do so. The President sent for his Secretary in my presence and told him to inform the State Government that he knew that the statue was ready and he would be arriving on Patna on 25 June to unveil it. The State Government need not worry about his security. He would be happy to meet his end at the feet of JP. The President kept his promise and arrived in Patna to unveil JP's statue before a crowd of a few lakhs. This was the first time that a President had visited a State at the invitation of a private individual against the wishes of the State Government. I had the immense satisfaction at seeing the President paying the Nation's tribute to JP on 25 June, the date in 1975 on which that great national icon was incarcerated.

4

INDIA'S FIRST FIELD MARSHAL

It was on New Year day of 1973 Nation got to know that the architect of India's greatest military victory in thousands of years of her history, had been elevated to the rank of Field Marshal. This came as a surprise to most of us. Only a couple of months earlier, the then Defence Minister had told the Press at Chennai that India would not have a Field Marshal or a five star General. I remember a friend of mine telling me at that time that if Pakistan had won the 1971 war, Yahya would have been made a Field Marshal the very next day. I disagreed with him saying that he would not have been made a Field Marshal but would have made himself one, like Ayub. My thoughts went back to 1946 when for the first time three Indian officers were posted to the Military Operations Directorate at Delhi, hitherto the exclusive preserve of British officers and British clerks. These were Lt Col Manekshaw, Major Yahya Khan and I in the rank of Captain. Who could then have predicted the path, careers of Manekshaw and Yahya would take? Inscrutable are the ways of providence.

I had the privilege of serving under Sam Manekshaw in all the ranks that he held from Lt Col to Army Chief. He had a tremendous capacity for work and he was a brilliant professional, contributing immensely in every appointment. He combined all this with a great sense of humour and ready wit. As a senior staff officer at Army Headquarters in 1971, I saw how meticulously he was planning for coming war, during nine month preparatory time, he had managed to obtain. The resounding victory that we achieved in that war was a crowning achievement of the foremost military leader of our Army.

I was functioning as Adjutant General, the Army's chief of personnel, in January 1973. I had to work out his entitlements in his new rank. I went to his office to congratulate him. I found him examining the badges of rank in cloth that had been prepared by Bastani Brothers, the tailor in South Block. Apparently Sam had been informed of his promotion a day or two earlier. To maintain secrecy, his personal staff told the tailor that a Nepalese Field Marshal was to come and his badge of rank had to be stitched. Sam told me that an investiture was to be held two days later at Rashtrapati Bhavan and I had to work out all the details with the Government. I replied that it would be both an honour and a pleasure to do so. However, I told him that the cloth badges of rank will be of no use. He would have to be in his ceremonial uniform for which he would need metal badges of rank. Moreover, the badges of rank made by the tailor were not correct. The Ashoka Lion at top of the wreath had to be in miniature; touching the top of the two loops in one badge of rank. He asked me how did I know this. I replied that when Auchinleck used to visit the Operations Room in 1946, I used to closely watch his badges of rank and ribbons. He said that he saw more of Auchinleck than me but he was not sure what I said was correct. He wanted something authentic. I went back to my office and tried to find out some written authority but nothing was available. I rang up our Military Attaché in London. He told me that the War Office was closed for Christmas holidays and he would not be able to send me anything for a week. I then thought of looking up the Encyclopedia Britanica. I was happy to find a coloured picture of a Field Marshal's badges of rank. That satisfied Sam. I said I would get them fabricated in the Army Workshop in Delhi Cantonment. Working round the clock our electrical engineers made a good job of it and completed the task within 24 hours.

We worked out a paper on the privileges Sam was now entitled to. A Field Marshal never retires. He would therefore be entitled to full pay for the rest of his life. He had to have a ceremonial baton which would now be part of his uniform. Besides, he would have to be given a small secretariat and personal staff. We also had to work out the procedure to be followed for the investiture at Rashtrapati Bhavan. A meeting was held, attended by Home Ministry officials, Additional Secretary Ministry of Defence and me with Home Secretary in the chair. Having been an old hand in Army Headquarters, I was fully aware of the hostility of the civilian bureaucracy towards the Army. I saw that in full force at this meeting. I found the Babudom opposing all our suggestions. They wanted the Cabinet Secretary, who was higher in protocol status to Sevice Chiefs to have a higher place than Sam in the seating plan. I maintained that a Field Marshal should rank with the awardees of Bharat Ratna. The latter enjoyed much higher protocol status than the Cabinet Secretary. In any case, irrespective of protocol status, Sam should have a special place sitting alone as an awardee. This was agreed to. There was heated debate regarding Fiekd Marshal's baton. The Babus considered one lakh as wasteful expenditure for the gold mounted Ashoka Lions on the baton. They pointed out that the five star Generals in the US Army do not have a baton. I replied that the Americans do not have Field Marshal. Frederick the Great had introduced the rank of Field Marshal as part of reforms in Prussian Army in the Eighteenth Century. A conquering General was not now allowed to keep any part of war booty. That was now to go to the State. Generals who had done exceptionally well in war, would be promoted Field Marshal which would entitle them to full salary for the rest of their life. That is how the tradition of a Field Marshal never retiring originated. The Field Marshal was also to be given a ceremonial baton like the monarch having an orb. His protocol status was to be next only to the monarch. Thus, originated the tradition of Regimental flags dipping in salute only for the monarchead of State and Field Marshal. They do not do so for Prime Ministers. Gradually all armies in Europe introduced this rank. UK was the last to do so. The Duke of Wellington captured a French Marshal's baton in Spain and sent it to his sovereign. He was made the first Field Marshal of the British

Army. Since the Government had decided to make Sam a Field Marshal, he must be given all the traditional privileges that go with that rank. I won my point on baton but not on other issues like salary or protocol status. In typical bureaucratic style it was decided to defer decision on them. In the interim, a meagerly sum of Rs 400 per month was approved as special pay, in addition to pension for Sam. A fortnight later, when Sam was demitting office, we had a ceremonial farewell parade for him on Army Day. For the first time, we brought Regimental flag on parade for the Army Day. I had kept it as a surprise for Sam. When he arrived for the parade, I mentioned this to him. He asked me in his usual manner, "Tell me sweety, how do I respond to the salute". He then took me by surprise. I did not know how a Field Marshal returns a salute. I later learnt that while doing so, British Field Marshals hold the baton in their Left hand at an angle of 45 degrees to the middle of their Left thigh. However, I had seen movies in which Reich Marshal Goring used to raise his baton in his Right hand. I promptly replied, "Sir, by raising the baton in your Right hand". Sam accepted this. We started a new tradition of our own.

Thirty two years later, I learnt from Press reports that consequent to the visit of President Abdul Kalam to Staff College Wellington when he met Sam, then terminally ill in the hospital. the Government had at long last taken a decision on the salary of a Field Marshal, the Defence Secretary flew to Wellington to personally hand over a cheque of Rs 1.3 crores to Sam as his arrears of pay for over thirty years. A couple of weeks later, I went to the Staff College to deliver a lecture. I met Sam in the hospital. I congratulated him for the arrears he had received. He replied, "Sweety, a Babu from Delhi came and gave me a cheque. I have sent it to the bank. I do not know if it will be honoured". That was the last time I met Sam. Soon after, Sam died. It was a national shame that we did not give him an appropriate funeral. As per our protocol, a Field Marshal ranks above the Service Chiefs and below the Cabinet Secretary. The Babudom had had its way. The Government was represented by a mere Minister of State at the funeral. The funeral should have taken place in Delhi with the President, Prime Minister and High Commissioner of Bangladesh or a high dignitary from that country, attending it. When Duke of Wellington died, several Monarchs, Presidents and Prime Ministers attended his funeral and he was buried in Westminster Abbey.

5

MOUNTBATTEN: AS I SAW HIM

Admiral of the Fleet, Earl Mountbatten of Burma was one of the most colourful personalities of twentieth century. He was gifted with almost everything in life, blue blood, good looks, professional ability and good fortune, which he put to good use in his meteoric career full of astounding achievements. His role as Viceroy and Governor General of India became controversial. I do not propose to go into that. I shall confine myself to recalling what little I saw of him, when I was a very junior army officer.

I recall on a bright clear day in February 1947, when John Spittle and I watched a long cavalcade of cars racing up the Raisina Hill from Central Vista (Now Vijay Chowk) to the Viceroy's House (now Rashtrapati Bhavan). A black limousine flying the Union Jack was prominent in the convoy. Mountbatten, the incoming Viceroy was travelling in that car. John was quite a few years older than me. He had been a school teacher for some time before being conscripted into British Army during the war. We both worked in the Operations Room of GHQ (now Army Headquarters) and had become good friends. We saw Mountbatten's convoy go past from the Operations Room on the first floor of South Block. John quoted the words of Queen Victoria inscribed on the arch over the entrance to North Block: "Liberty will not descend upon a people. A people must raise themselves to liberty that must be earned before it can be enjoyed". He said that the independence of India was in the air and it was in the fitness of things that the great grandson of the great Queen had come to grant independence to India. I did not want to raise acrimony by saying that independence would be coming to us as a compulsion of the post world war scenario and not as an act of bounty. I reminded him of Churchill had said that he had not become King's first Minister to preside over the liquidation of British Empire. And now Mountbatten, a protégé of Churchill who had appointed him Supreme Commander during the war, had come to preside over the Empire's liquidation. John laughed and said that no doubt Mountbatten had been Churchill's blue eyed boy. Three Service Chiefs in South East Asia were all several years senior to Mountbatten. His royal connection was expected to make him acceptable, not only to them but also to Americans. General Joe Stillwell known as Vinegar Joe, commanding the American and Chinese forces in the theatre, was a difficult person to work with. He was appointed Deputy Supreme Commander. No Hollywood star in an Admiral's uniform, could be as striking as Mountbatten. He shook hands with a dazzling smile and Vinegar Joe's resistance melted in the glow of his personality. John added that he had then been sent by Atlee to India to mesmerize Indians with his charm and to overwhelm the feudal Princes with his royal lineage. Neither John nor I could then foresee that in less than six months, the country would suffer a holocaust of unprecedented dimension and will be partitioned into two separate sovereign dominions. Partition was announced on 3 June 1947. The next day a special calendar was issued to be put up in all offices of Government of India. It showed two dates 15 August and the actual date, with the number of days to Partition on each page.

I had served in Burma and Indonesia during the war, when Mountbatten was the Supreme Commander. I had my first glimpse of him in Singapore in March 1946. Jawaharlal Nehru was visiting Singapore at the invitation of the Indian community. He held no official position at that time. Thousands of Indians and Chinese had gone to Changi airport to receive him. I was surprised to see a number of Indian soldiers in Army trucks with Congress flags at the airport. This had never happened before. I was now convinced that India's independence was round the corner. I saw a British Colonel go to the tarmac at the airport to receive Nehru. I was told he was the Military

Secretary of Mountbatten. He saluted Nehru and took him in an army staff car to the Government House, where Mountbatten was staying. Nehru was to lay the foundation stone of a new memorial for the Indian National Army. The old memorial was dynamited by British soldiers after Singapore was recaptured. Nehru was also to visit Indonesia at the invitation of Soekarno. At that time, the Indian Army was fighting Soekarno's force and Biju Patnaik was doing gun running for him. We learnt that Mountbatten switched on his charm on Nehru and persuaded him to give up both these engagements. He told him that India would soon be independent and he should not do anything that would impair the discipline of the Indian Army. That was the first time that the two had met and this was the beginning of their long friendship. The following day Mountbatten took Nehru with him to the Army canteen for a cup of tea with the soldiers. There was tremendous enthusiasm amongst the soldiers on seeing them. That was the first time I got a glimpse of Mountbatten.

I saw Mountbatten from close quarters on the second occasion. I was on duty in the Operations Room at the Corps Headquarters in Batavia, now Jakarta. Mountbatten walked into the Operations Room along with Corps Commander, Lt Gen Sir Montagu Stopford. My boss, Colonel Stevens briefed him on the map. During the briefing, Mountbatten said that he wanted to talk to Maj Gen Robert Mansergh, commanding the Division at Sourabaya. I was asked to put a call to him on the hotline. I rang up the Division's Operations Room and spoke to my counterpart Bill Cunningham. I asked him to get his General on the line for the Supremo. I knew Bill well and we often spoke to each other on the telephone. He said OK and after a pause, when I heard a gruff voice saying Yes, I said, "General Mansergh is on the line Sir". Mountbatten picked up the receiver and said, "Mountbatten here. Is that you Bob?" The voice at the other end replied "If you are Mountbatten, I am Montgomery". Mountbatten smiled and said "Would someone convince him that I am Mountbatten". Cunningham had thought that I was pulling his leg. Colonel Stevens now took the telephone and spoke sharply to him to get his GOC on the line. Thereafter Mountbatten talked to Mansergh and then left. I was ticked off by my Colonel saying that I should have made sure that General Mansergh was on the line before handing over the receiver. Bill Cunningham also got away lightly. Later in the day, Mountbatten addressed all officers in the station. Sitting next to me was Mohammad Nawaz also a Captain at our Headquarters. He later joined the civil service and ended up as Cabinet Secretary in Pakistan. Also present in the audience was Capt Niazi from the Rajput Regiment in the station. He later became a Lt Gen in Pakistan Army and surrendered with 90,000 Pakistani soldiers to us at Dacca in 1971. I was overall in charge of these prisoners and I met him again a few times. Mountbatten's address was flamboyant but we were all very impressed. He told us that soon after he took over as Supreme Commander, he went to Cairo to present his plans for offensive in South East Asia to the Big Three, Roosevelt, Churchill and Stalin. The British Army Chief, Alanbrooke, who was also present, remarked that it was dangerous to have Admirals on land. Mountbatten promptly retorted not as dangerous as Generals at sea. He was happy that his plans had succeeded and South East Asia had been liberated from the Japanese. He then went on to tell us that his command both in territory and population was much larger than that of the other two Supreme Commanders, MacArthur and Eisenhower. Whereas the war was over elsewhere, in South East Asia, we were still fighting in Indo-China and Indonesia. Its outcome will determine the future of Asia he had concluded. I wondered whether while talking of Indo-China and Indonesia, he had India in mind for the new world order emerging in Asia.

Hukum Singh Yadav, whom we called Kim was a good friend of mine. He was appointed ADC to Mountbatten when he took over as Viceroy. I heard interesting stories of the Mountbatten household from him. Mountbatten was very particular about his dress and his looks. He was referred to as the "matinee idol with nice eye lashes". He had a barber on his staff from Trumpers saloon near Piccadily Circus in London. After he dressed up whether in uniform or civilian clothes, the ADC was required to examine him from head to foot and from different angles. He would ask, "How do I look? The ADC would answer, "Excellent, Your Excellency". Kim became friendly with Ann, the Secretary of Lady Mountbatten. The two got married and lived happily for the rest of their lives. Alas, both are now no more. Kim gave a wedding reception at swimming pool in the Viceroy's House, which I attended. The Mountbattens dropped in for a short while. Mixed marriages were frowned upon in those days. Mountbattens showed that they had no inhibitions on that score.

While Mountbatten was Viceroy, I had glimpses of him on a few occasions. On Independence Day, I saw him going down The Kingsway (now Rajpath) in a horse carriage with Nehru. The cheering crowd was delirious shouting "Pandit Nehru ki Jay, Pandit Mountbatten ki Jay". As they arrived at the site of the parade, the crowd broke the cordon and engulfed the troops lined up for the parade. No parade could be held. However the band struck the national anthem and our new national flag, the tricolor, was unfurled. Kim told me that Mountbatten had said it was the best parade he had seen in his life. Mountbatten held a Reception in the newly designated Governor General's House, later to be called Rashtrapati Bhavan. A Major in the Army still figured in the Warrant of Precedence. I along with several Majors and numerous senior dignitaries attended the Reception. There were about a thousand guests. Mountbattens in their regalia stood in the hall and shook hands with each guest. This was a tremendous display of their physical stamina. I also attended the farewell function held at Delhi Gymkhana Club for the departing British and Pakistani officers. Major General Cariappa promoted to that rank on Independence Day and Indian officers were the hosts at the function. Admiral Sir Andrew Fraser, the C-in-C of the Eastern Fleet based at Trincomalee and his wife were also our guests. As Mountbatten arrived, the band played the national anthem. While shaking hands with Mountbatten, Sir Andrew Fraser bowed and Lady Fraser did a courtesy. This is done only for the ucovereign or someone representing the ucovereign him.. Fraser was about ten years senior in service to Mountbatten. He was a four star Admiral while Mountbatten was still in his two star substantive rank. In 1948, he reverted to the Navy in his substantive rank and commanded the cruiser squadron in the Mediterranean, while Fraser became the First Sea Lord as Chief of the Royal Navy. It took a few years for Mountbatten to work his way up and become not only the First Sea Lord but also Admiral of the Fleet, the naval equivalent for Field

Marshal. Subsequently he became Chief of Defence Staff, an appointment recently introduced in Britain. He Successded the first incumbent of that appointment, an Air Chief Marshal who did a short stint.

In late August 1947, law and order situation in Delhi and all over North India had become critical. One afternoon we in Military Operations at Army HQ were told that an operations room had to be set up in the Governor General's House. This had to be completed by the following morning for a cabinet meeting. Mountbatten was rushing back from Simla to Delhi that evening. Manekshaw had just been promoted full Colonel and was now our Deputy Director. He took me and another officer with a couple of clerks and draftsmen to the Governor General's House. He explained to us what had to be done. We had to put up a few maps showing troop locations and incidents of violence as also progress in evacuation of refugees. It was a herculean task and we had to work through the night. We were well looked after with coffee and sandwiches by the Governor General's staff. Manekshaw came in the morning and checked our work. A little later Mountbatten with his Military Secretary, Douglas Currie arrived. He saw the maps and was satisfied with our work. He asked Currie, "I hope these officers did not starve while working here". Currie replied that we had been well looked after. He then turned round to us and said "Well done". In 1972, Manekshaw was the Army Chief and I was a Major General on his staff. Larrie Collins and Dominique Lapiere had come to Delhi for collecting material for a book they were writing. Manekshaw asked me to brief them about what had happened in 1947 and show them round the various sites in Delhi connected with the events of that time. Among various other places I also showed them the room in Rashtrapati Bhavan where we had set up the Operations Room. In their book, Freedom at Midnight, they wrote that Nehru and Patel asked Mountbatten to come down from Simla to help them manage the critical situation in the country. They also wrote that Mountbatten used to preside over cabinet meetings, which a constitutional Head of State was not supposed to do. This became a controversial issue. Some people wrote in the newspapers, contradicting the version of these two authors.

In 1961, I attended the Joint Services Staff College at

Latimer near London, an institution recently established at Mountbatten's initiative when he was appointed CDS. It was a combined integrated course for officers of the three Services who had earlier graduated from their respective Service Staff College. It was half way between Service Staff College and the Imperial Defence College. The Joint Services Staff College has now been redesignated National Defence College and Imperial Defence College as Royal College of Defence Studies. The students at Latimer were mostly from the British Services and a good number from other NATO countries. There were also two students from Pakistan and one from India. Mountbatten, the then CDS came to address our course. He spoke in his flamboyant style and much impressed us all. He started his talk with a reference to his father Lord Battenberg, who had been the First Sea Lord at the start of the First World War. He had to resign on account of his German name and German connection. It was Mountbatten's ambition to redeem his father's honour by reaching the top in the Royal Navy. They were the only father son duo in the history of the Royal Navy to become the First Sea Lord. Mountbatten also went on to become Admiral of the Fleet, equivalent of Field Marshal, and Chief of Defence Staff. He told us that as a child, he sat on his father's knees and asked him the reason for the supremacy of the Royal Navy. His father told him that the Royal Navy should be kept twice as strong as any other Navy in the world. When he became the First Sea Lord, Royal Navy was half the size of major navies of the world. This underscored the need for joint functioning of three Services which is an imperative of modern warfare. Each Service had to give up its inhibitions. When he took over as CDS, he found that in the name of tradition, each Service was finding it difficult to change its functioning style. The Navy quoted the Battle of Trafalgar, the Army the Battle of Waterloo and the Air Force not to be left out, the Battle of Britain. As Chief of Combined Operations, he had been a member of the Chiefs of Staff Committee during the early years of the Second World War. At that tine inaumbant three Service Chiefs were serving in the rank of Lt Col or equivalent. This along with the fact that he had been a Supreme Commander, had helped him to get them to co-operate in developing the required inter-service ethos. In India he had introduced a common cadet academy for the three Services at Pune, which was the first of its kind in the world. He also had a common staff college established. Each Service had its separate staff course. Their syllabus also included some periods devoted to joint training for the three Services. Before Second World War, the Army had a two years staff course, Navy six months and Air Force one year. He told us that there was some problem in a common duration one year staff course for all. He had heard that at the Indian Staff College at Wellington, the Army got no week ends, Air Force got all week ends and Navy was on permanent week end. Continuing in a lighter vein, he said that he had heard that in UK there was a different approach to training at the three grades of Staff College. At Service Staff College in Greenwich, Camberley and Bracknell, questions were asked and if the students did not know the answers, they were bowled out. At the Joint Services Staff College, they did not mind if the students did not know the answer but at the Imperial Defence College they did not ask questions because they were sure that the students did not know the answers. After cracking these jokes, he advised us to work hard and take full advantage of the opportunity available to us to imbibe inter-service training and inter-service ethos.

There was a reception in the evening at the College that evening for Mountbatten. The prescribed dress for the function was dinner jacket and black tie. I chose to wear my black sherwani. I was the only Indian at the function. Soon after his arrival Mountbatten spotted me and came straight to me, possibly as a gesture to identify himself with India. He told me, "You look like Pandit Nehru". I realized he was referring to my dress and not my looks. I replied, "Sir, I do not have a red rose". He then said, "In Britain we had a war of roses before the Tudors came to power. Make sure that you do not have a war of roses in India". That was the last time I saw Mountbatten or interacted with him.

In 1979, I was a Lt Gen holding the appointment of chief of personnel of the Army. One day the British Military Attache came to see me in my office. He told me that Mountbatten was upset because for over three months, he had not received any reply or even acknowledgment to his letter to our Defence Minister. I inquired from him the subject matter of the letter.

He said that Mountbatten was planning arrangements for his own funeral. It had been decided that the function would take place in Westminster Abbey. He wanted to know whether the Defence Services of India will participate in that function. I assured the Attache that I would look into the matter and get back to him soon. Normally such a letter should have come to me to put up a draft reply. I had not received any such letter. I checked with the Ministry of Defence but and they were not aware of any such letter. I then spoke to Jagjivan Ram, the then Defence Minister. He recalled that such a letter had come. A search was launched in his Secretariat and the letter was traced. It had got misplaced. Soon I received an envelope addressed to Mountbatten which I was required to hand over to the British Military Attache for onward dispatch. I also got the office copy of the letter for my record. It was a very tactful reply personally drafted by Jagjivan Ram. He wrote to Mountbatten that he had received his letter some time back but he did not have the heart to send him a reply. In India it is considered bad omen to discuss the funeral arrangements for a living person. He was much loved in India and there was no question of the Armed Forces of India not participating in his funeral. However, he prayed that the occasion for that did not arise for many many years to come. I handed over this letter to the British Military Attache. It so happened that within a couple of months, Mountbatten was holidaying in Ireland. He went out to the sea in a small boat. The IRA had planted a bomb in that boat which exploded off the coast of Dublin, killing Mountbatten. A contingent of the Indian Armed Forces led by Admiral Periera, the then Naval Chief, participated in his funeral.

6

A SOLDIER DIPLOMAT

There is a saying that when a lady says No, she means May Be, when she says May Be, she means Yes and if she says Yes, she is not a lady. The saying for a diplomat is that when he says Yes, he means May Be, when he says May Be, he means No and if he says No, he is not a diplomat. I served in the Army for forty years. After I quit the Army, I was appointed India's Ambassador to Nepal. I wondered how a soldier should fit into this scheme of things. I decided to work out a formula of my own. I asserted that when a soldier says Yes, he means Yes, when he says No, he means No and when he says May Be, he is not a soldier.

It is our tradition in the Army that a regimental officer identifies himself with his men not only by learning their language but also by establishing close personal relations with them. Field Marshal Slim, a veteran Gorkha officer wrote that a regimental officer should know his men better than their mothers do and care for them no less. As a young officer in the Gorkhas, I tried to live up to that ideal. During my leave, I used to trek to Pokhra and surrounding areas from where our soldiers came. This was with a view to meet their families and the ex-servicemen from my regiment. This cemented my bonds with my men. When I took over as Director of Military Intelligence at Army Headquarters, I gave this a stamp of official approval. I provided intelligence funds for regimental teams to go on long treks to Nepal and these treks were now treated as official duty and did not eat into anyone's leave. When I became the

Adjutant General, I further strengthened this arrangement by also providing welfare funds to the regimental teams which were now also supplemented by medical teams with stocks of medicine. Besides, I undertook several other special measures for the welfare of Gorkha troops. These included setting up a special cell (PS-10) in Adjutant General's Branch for Gorkhas, acquiring land at Pokhra as Deputy Adjutant General in 1972 and later as Adjutant General attending the inauguration of the Pokhra Pension Paying Camp in 1978 by our then Ambassador in Kathmandu. I started an ambitious project enlisting the support of both Ministries of Defence and of External Affairs for a Bhartiya Gorkha Sainik Nivas at Kathmandu. I had the privilege to inaugurate it when I took over as Ambassador in Nepal. The British Army Chief on a visit to Nepal stated that he had not seen a better rest house for ex-servicemen anywhere in the world. I also set up a Gorkha Resettlement Training Unit at Raiwalla in Dehradun. Gorkha soldiers while still in service attended courses of their choice at that unit in the last year of their service to equip them for a career in Nepal after retirement. Apart from being Colonel of my regiment, I was also the President of the Gorkha Brigade. During my tenures of two to three years each as Deputy Adjutant General and Adjutant General, I made several official visits to Nepal. All this enabled me to be familiar with Nepal. I may in all humility add that I had come to be regarded as a good friend of Nepal.

In early 1989 the Trade and Transit Treaty between India and Nepal was allowed to lapse. There had been some personal misunderstandings between King Birendra of Nepal and Prime Minister Rajiv Gandhi on trivial issues. Hardliners on both sides had their way. On the Indian side the feeling was that this would make Nepal come down on her knees and on the Nepalese side they wanted to show that they could manage without any assistance from India. International obligations required India to provide at least one trade and transit point to a land locked country. India had provided two such points at Raxaul in Central and Biratnagar in Eastern Nepal. Previously, there were 22 trade and transit points between the two countries. In view of poor lateral communications within Nepal, the country's western part was badly affected. This region is the home of the bulk of Gorkha soldiers serving in the Indian Army. There was acute shortage of kerosene and salt in the villages of West Nepal. Despite the grave hardships being faced by their families in West Nepal, the Gorkha soldier serving in Siachen Glacier or in Sri Lanka never wavered in his loyalty to India. The hardliners in India found that Nepal could manage to survive albeit with great setback to her economy and suffering great hardships. She faced acute shortages of various commodities. Petrol was strictly rationed and there were long queues at petrol stations. There was much international sympathy for Nepal on account of a so called economic blockade by India. The controversy was viewed as a struggle between David and Goliath, Nepal being the former and India the latter. The hardliners in Nepal found that there was no alternative to India for Nepal. Goods in adequate quantity could not be brought in by air nor overland from Tibet. India and Nepal were entwined too closely both in terms of geography and economy. Li Peng the Chinese Prime Minister on a visit to Kathmandu put this across succinctly by advising Nepal to come to terms with her geography. Apart from the economic crisis facing Nepal there was also a major political crisis raging in that country. For some time the people were agitating against Panchayat Raj in the country which was a euphemism for royal dictatorship. Multi party system was banned. Ultimate power rested with the King who nominated the Prime Minister and the Ministers. The political parties, namely Nepali Congress and Nepali Communist party had got together and formed a Restoration of Democracy Front with the veteran Congressman Ganesh Man Singh, as their Supreme Leader. They started a countrywide agitation for restoration of democracy. All the leaders of the movement were imprisoned by the King but the agitation was continuing.

I had gone to our two daughters in the USA for a couple of months when the trade and transit treaty lapsed. Indo-Nepal relations had hit an all time low. I started receiving letters from ex-servicemen in Nepal to do something to alleviate their hardship. As a retired officer not in the good books of the ruling Congress Government, I was hardly in a position to do anything in the matter. I felt sad and helpless. Providence has its own way of ordaining things. Little could I then realize that Destiny would soon put me in a key position to resolve this grave issue. Soon after I returned to India, parliamentary elections were held and Rajiv Gandhi Government was voted out of power. VP Singh took over as Prime Minister and within three days of assuming his appointment, he sent for me. I had met VP Singh a few times earlier but I was in no way close to him. I was surprised to receive his summon. When I met him in his office, he told me that he had two major problems on his hand, Kashmir internally and Nepal externally. In view of my long association with Kashmir from Day One that is, 27 October 1947, Ministry of Home wanted me to go as Governor to Kashmir. Similarly on account of my long association with Gorkhas and the work I had been doing in Nepal, Ministry of External Affairs wanted me to go as our Ambassador to Nepal. Although I preferred the latter, I told the Prime Minister that I left the choice to him. He thought for a minute and then said that I should go to Kashmir immediately. I told him that I would need to go to my home in Patna for three or four days for packing before proceeding to Kashmir. He said that was no problem. The following day I received a telephone call in Patna from the External Affairs Minister that an alternative had been found for Kashmir and the Prime Minister now wanted me to go to Nepal. I was delighted at this change. However, Destiny has its own ways. Thirteen years later, I was appointed as Governor of Jammu and Kashmir and that is a different story.

At a time when Indo-Nepal relations had reached their nadir and when there were reports of anti-India demonstrations in front of the Indian Embassy at Kathmandu, I faced a grave challenge as India's Ambassador in Nepal. I had certain advantages which an Ambassador does not normally have. I had a popular image among over 1,00,000 Gorkha ex-servicemen in Nepal. I was well known among the Nepalese for the work I had been doing in Nepal. My other assets apart from ability to speak in Nepali were my close political and army connections. BP Koirala the father of democracy in Nepal had lived in exile in Patna for a few years when I was a College student. He was a close friend of my uncle and lived in a house adjacent to his. I used to often meet him and several Nepalese Congress leaders who used to visit him. Four decades later, when I quit the Army and went back to Patna, I developed very cordial relations with Devendra Prasad Singh, a family friend. He had a Nepalese wife and GP Koirala used to often come and stay with him.

Devendra was a close colleague of BP Koirala and in the Sixties had done gun running for Nepali Congress during their struggle against the Rana regime. On his visits to Patna, GP Koirala had come to my house a few times. My army connection was also an asset in my new assignment. I had been an instructor at Mhow and at Wellington for three years each. Several officers of Royal Nepal Army had done training courses at these two training institutions when I was an instructor there. The Chief of Nepal Army and all his Pricipal Staff Officers had been my student at either Mhow or Wellington. This was a strong bond. Yet some elements among the intelligentsia who had an anti-India mindset showed reservations about me. It came out in the Nepalese Press that for the first time India had sent an army officer as Ambassador to Nepal. This showed India's militaristic designs for establishing hegemony over Nepal !

When I arrived in Nepal, the country was under a royal dictatorship. The King was all powerful and the fountain head of authority in every sphere of governance. The common man revered him as the incarnation of Lord Vishnu and the Army, specially its senior officers, was intensely loyal to him. Political leaders agitating for a multi party democracy had been placed behind bars. Normally an Ambassador on arrival waited for weeks before presenting his credentials. Generally two or more new Ambassadors were clubbed together for presentation of credentials. In a rare departure from normal practice, I was invited the day after I arrived in Kathmandu to present my credentials. This was perhaps on account of the economic crisis facing Nepal, for resolving which Indian assistance was vital.

After I presented my credentials and the formal function was over, the King invited me for a drink. The Prime Minister and Foreign Minister also joined us. The King started conversation with me in English, saying "Your Excellency, Mr Rajiv Gandhi started talking to us through the Press and that is how the relations between our countries soured. They say that we are anti-India. India is such a large country and we are such a small country. How can we afford to be anti-India". I replied in my chaste Nepali, "Your Majesty, there is a new Government in Delhi now which accords the highest priority to having the most cordial relations with your country. As a proof of their intention, they have sent me here because of my very long and cordial relations with your subjects serving in the Indian Army and also those who have retired. India being large and Nepal being small, is a fact of geography. There is also another fact of geography. Nepal is at the head of the Indian Sub-Continent. The head is much smaller than the rest of the body". The King laughed heartily and said that for the first time he had an Ambassador who spoke his language. He wanted to have a long chat with me. Prime Minister and Foreign Minister withdrew. I stayed on with the King for nearly an hour. He was interested to know about my earlier visits to his country, my relations with Gorkha soldiers and the welfare work for the soldiers and pensioners of the Indian Army that I had been doing in Nepal. I told him how in the old days when there was no road to Pokhra and no air service, I had trekked along the mountain tracks halting at Bhattis (pubs) run by Thakalnis (women of Thakal tribe known for their beauty). I even repeated to him the words of some Nepalese songs which I used to sing to the madal (two sided Nepalese drum) on the line of march with my soldiers. He was much amused when I gave him the words of a popular song, "Thakalni ko paelo galo, aunda janda Laure le maikhala" (The Thakalni has yellow cheeks which the soldier kisses while travelling up and down). After an hour of friendly and informal conversation, the King breaking all protocol came out of the Palace to my car to see me off. He told me that I was welcome to see him whenever I wanted. He would instruct his staff to arrange audience for me. This was a tremendous change from what had been happening earlier. My predecessor wanting an audience with him had not been given one for over a year because of strained Indo-Nepal relations.

I took full advantage of King's friendly attitude towards me. I was having an audience with him almost every fortnight. I had made a good start but I had to endeavour hard to persuade him to promote democracy and restore normalcy in the country. This was not an easy task. I had to ensure that the King did not feel that I was interfering in the internal affairs of his country. I was given to understand that the Chinese Ambassador had told him that they had successfully quelled a democratic movement at Tinamen Square. The King could similarly quell the movement for democracy in Nepal. It was also suggested that the Chinese troops next door in Tibet could help if required. The Queen was much under the influence of the Chinese and had been warning the King against getting close to India. There were reports that on one occasion, she had thrown a teapot filled with tea at the King. I talked to the King about my experience of dealing with armed insurgency of the Nagas and Mizos in North East India. Armed insurgency had also commenced then in Kashmir. After some time, when I felt that I had won the confidence of the King, I mentioned to him that the movement for democracy in Nepal simmering in the country was gaining momentum. The agitators were demanding constitutional monarchy in Nepal. If a settlement was not reached with them, it would not be long before they would ask for abolition of monarchy. I reminded him that in Sixties, the agitation against the Rana regime had been violent, with armed insurgents operating from bases across the border in India. The Rana regime had got overthrown. If the ongoing movement in Nepal became an armed insurgency, the Government would find it difficult to deal with it. India with all her resources was finding it difficult to tackle insurgency in the North East and in Kashmir. Nepal with limited resources and a 1700 mile open border with India will find it ever more difficult to do so. The King would listen to my views carefully but would remain non-committal.

The agitation for democracy continued to gather momentum. Apart from striking students there was teachers strike and even Government servants struck work. There was a ban on holding public meetings in Nepal. The King decided to relax the ban and a public meeting was allowed to be held in Kathmandu on 6 April 1990. Several thousand people attended the meeting at which demand for introduction of multi-party democracy was Vehemently made. After the meeting, a large crowd numbering a few thousand rushed towards Singh Durbar, the Nepal Government Secretariat. The Police had to open fire and some demonstrators were killed. The agitators reassembled and now moved threateningly towards the King's Palace. The Army was called out and it resorted to repeated firing on agitators in the city. Never before in recent memory, had Khathmandu witnessed such large scale violence. From the Embassy I could hear rifle firing and the siren of ambulance vehicles. A few agitated Indians and Nepalese rang me up in the Embassy saying hat the Government was committing large scale genocide. They wanted the Indian Army to be brought to Kathmandu by air next morning to stop the massacre of the people. I realized that the situation had become very serious but I could not in any circumstance recommend the Indian Army getting involved in Nepal. That would have had far more serious repercussion than our ill advised recent military intervention in Sri Lanka. Very late that night, the Foreign Minister, Pashupati Rana came to see me in the Embassy with a message from the King. They knew that I was in touch with Nepali Congress leaders. They wanted me to mediate so that a settlement could be reached. I told Pashupati that my mediating would be misunderstood as people may criticise it as India's intervention in Nepal's internal affairs. He saw my point. I suggested to him that the Government should announce four steps – release all political prisoners, institute inquiry into excesses by security forces, announce framing of a new constitution and install an interim government of leaders of Nepali Congress and Nepali Communist party, pending the holding of elections under a new constitution. I assured him that these proposals will be acceptable to leaders of the movement for democracy. I would do my bit to ensure that they accept them. I also told him that this would be on the lines of what the British had done in India in 1946 when an interim coalition government of the Congress and the Muslim League had been installed. The King accepted these suggestions and the following day all the political leaders were released. There was tremendous jubilation in Nepal. I met Ganeshman Singh, KP Bhattarai, and GP Koirala. They were all in high spirits. The next day an interim coalition government was sworn in with Bhattarai as Prime Minister and Sohana Pradhan from Communist Party as Deputy Prime Minister. Ganeshman Singh, the supreme leader of the movement remained out of the Government and so did GP Koirala President of the Nepali Congress and Manmohan Adhikari, the top leader of Nepali Communist Party.

I was happy that democracy had been restored in Nepal and I could now work on getting the trade and transit points with India reopened. Without a popular Government in Kathmandu, the hardliners in Delhi would not have been amenable to this. Soon after the interim government came to power, a major crisis erupted. Party cadres of the two political parties in power attacked policemen as revenge for atrocities committed by Policemen during the agitation. Six policemen were lynched. Nepal Police mutinied and there was widespread unrest. Control over the Army had remained with the King and without the King's support the Government was in no position to subdue the Police mutiny. The Prime Minister sought my help to resolve the crisis. I met the King and told him that history would remember him for restoring democracy in Nepal. Today that democracy was threatened and required his assistance to survive. He was widely revered in the country and an appeal by him on the television to maintain peace will help the Government to tide over the crisis without the Army being called out to restore order. I also told him how in Spain after the death of General Franco, democracy got restored. Soon thereafter democracy was in peril due to the military coup of the Colonels. The King of Spain intervened and saved democracy in that country. The King listened to my advice. That evening, he addressed the Nation on the television. This had a salutary effect. The Police mutiny was called off.

There was also a protocol problem that had to be resolved. As part of the feudal legacy of the past, the King always addressed Nepalese citizens irrespective of their status as Tum (Timi in Nepal) and not the polite Aap (Afu in Nepali). He also did not offer a chair to any Nepalese during audience with him. The Prime Minister resented this. He requested me to convey to the King that such old feudal practices were out of place in modern times. I mentioned this to the King and he said that he would look into it. Of course, since I was not a Nepalese, he would show me all the courtesies in conversation and would always offer me a chair. The next time the Prime Minister went to see the King he was offered a chair but the King spoke to him in English in which the word you is used both for an inferior and in polite conversation. The Nepalese Press brought out an interesting news item. It wrote that the King speaks with the Prime Minister in English and with the Indian Ambassador in Nepali.

I recommended to the Government of India that the trade and transit points should be opened as quickly as possible and generous economic aid be provided to Nepal so that its economy be revived from the ill effects of the closure of those points. I was asked to extend an invitation to the Prime Minister to visit Delhi for resolving these problems. Bhattarai agreed to visit Delhi provided he could return with an agreement on opening of the trade and transit points. His position in Nepal would get compromised if he went to Delhi and did not succeed in doing so. I assured him that we would get all the 22 transit points reopened. I conveyed all this to Delhi. I also told Delhi that we should arrange a generous aid package for Nepal. India was giving several crores for Aid Africa Fund. Nepal mattered much more to India than Africa. We should provide more funds for Nepal. The bureaucracy in Ministry of Extrenal Affairs was inclined to continue with the hardline approach of the past towards Nepal. I drafted an Indo-Nepal agreement and sent its copy to the Ministry. With their approval, I showed it to the Prime Minister and again assured him that all the transit points would get opened after his visit to Delhi. He issued a statement to the Press stating that the ongoing economic crisis in the country would get resolved after his visit to India and if that did not happen, he would resign.

I preceded the Prime Minister to Delhi by a day to help in preparing for his talks in India. I was horrified to learn that despite my proposals agreed to by the Ministry of External Affairs, they had now taken a contrary stand. I was told that it would not be possible for the Government of India at that stage to approve all the suggestions made by me in the draft agreement that I had prepared. For the present, some of the recommendations would be accepted and the remainder would be agreed upon when an elected Government came to power after a new Constitution was framed. It was felt that if we agreed to everything now then we would have little leverage while negotiating with an elected government when it came to power. I was also told that a paper on these lines had been prepared which had been sent by Gujral, the then External Affairs Minister to Prime Minister VP Singh and approved by the latter. In view of this, no change could now be made. I felt let down. With the approval of the Ministry I had conveyed to the Nepalese Prime Minister that all the 22 transit points would get reopened and now the stand being taken by Delhi was that only a few would be opened, the remainder to be opened later when a new treaty was signed with an elected Government of Nepal. I told the Foreign Secretary that in that case it would not be possible for me to continue as Ambassador in view of the assurance I had given to the Nepalese Prime Minister with the approval of Delhi. I offered to resign. I was told that my resigning during the visit of the Nepalese delegation to Delhi will cause much embarrassment. It was even mildly mentioned that I was blackmailing the authorities in Delhi. I met Gujral and he was quick to see my point of view. He agreed that the commitment made by me to the Prime Minister of Nepal had to be honoured. He assured me that he would revise his recommendation to VP Singh and get him to approve the same. Another hurdle arose during the course of official level talks. The Nepalese officials were opposed to dropping the newly introduced work permits for Indians in Nepal and re-employment of Indian teachers dismissed by the previous regime. I had informally discussed these points in my talks with Bhattarai in Nepal and he had agreed. It appeared that the Deputy Prime Minister Sohana Pradhan and the Nepalese bureaucrats had different views and the official talks had got stalled. At an after dinner meeting I urged Bhattarai staying at Rashtrapati Bhavan to overrule his delegation on these and some other issues. I told him of the very generous aid package for Nepal that had been worked out. I also reminded him that the failure of the ongoing talks would embarrass him. He had announced in Nepal that he would resign if he did not get all the 22 transit points reopened. He saw my point and agreed to overrule his delegation on the issues in dispute. I reported my conversation with Bhattarai to Gujral at midnight. He told me to invite Bhattarai for breakfast at VP Singh's residence the next morning. He felt that before Bhattarai under pressure from his delegation changed his mind we should get the joint statement of the two Prime Ministers approved. Much of the work on the joint statement had already been done and finishing touches to them were completed during the night. The aid package for Nepal in the statement was much more than the Nepalese had expected. The following morning, joint statement of the two Prime Ministers was finalised at the breakfast meeting in VP Singh's house, attended by Bhattarai, Gujral and me. A joint Press Conference was held at Delhi that afternoon. I accompanied Bhattarai the next day to Kathmandu. Details of the accord had come out on the electronic media the previous evening and in the newspaper that morning. A tumultuous reception awaited Bhattarai at the Tribhuvan airport and slogans were raised in support of Indo-Nepal friendship. I felt a tremendous sense of satisfaction at the favourable course of events.

I worked out an elaborate plan for opening all the trade and transit points with a lot of fanfare. Ministers/senior officials from the two sides were to be present at a formal function at each of the 22 points. Nautunwa in West Nepal near Gorakhpur was chosen as the main site for the functions. Mulayam Singh Yadav, the then Chief Minister of UP represented India at that site. Bhattarai and I went there from Kathmandu. I got the brass band of 11 Gorkha Centre at Lucknow to play at the function. A decorative arch with the flags of India and Nepal was put up at the border. One hundred vehicles flying flags of both countries and loaded with essential supplies like petrol, kerosene, sugar, salt and other commodities were lined up on the Indian side. 200 Gorkha ex-servicemen of the Indian Army wearing their medals lined up the road on the Nepalese side. There were nice hoardings of Indo-Nepal friendship put up on both sides. At the appointed time Bhattarai and Mulayam Singh cut the tape at the border. The national anthems of the two countries were played. A large crowd of local people from either side witnessed the function. This was followed by a public meeting addressed by Bhattarai, Mulayam Singh and me. In the evening fireworks were organized along with variety entertainment. On a miniature scale, similar functions were organized at all the other transit points. The function was covered live on Nepal television and got wide publicity in the Press. There was a groundswell of friendly feeling for India in Nepal. Attenborough's film Gandhi was shown in all countries of the world except Pakistan and Nepal. It was understandable that Pakistan placed an embargo on it but for Nepal to do so was very strange. I recall that during Quit India movement of 1942, Nepalese leaders like BP Koirala and Manmohan Adhikari then in India, had gone to jail along with Indian Congress leaders. The bitterness in the wake of a so called blockade of Nepal by India had led to Nepal Government putting a ban on the

Gandhi film. The situation had now changed dramatically. The film was now being shown in cinema halls packed to capacity all over Nepal.

I recall a public meeting at Kathmandu on Buddha Purnima addressed by the Prime Minister. This has been an annual feature in Nepal. All the then eighteen Ambassadors in Nepal attended the meeting. After Bhattarai had spoken, I was asked to address the audience of 30,000. This was the first time that an Ambassador had been asked to address such a meeting. Since it was a meeting in memory of the Great Enlightened One, who attained enlightenment in India and commenced giving sermons there, it was only in the fitness of things that the Indian Ambassador be invited to speak on that occasion. As I commenced my speech in Nepali, I received a thunderous applause from the audience. I told them that Buddha was born in Nepal, attained enlightenment in India and enriched humanity and the world with his haloed sermons from India. I added that today we have a person born and educated in India who has attained power in Nepal and is destined to take Nepal to great heights of prosperity and Indo-Nepal relations to unmatched levels of cordiality. I was referring to Bhattarai who was born in Varanasi and educated in Benares Hindu University. This also drew much applause. After the meeting, Bhattarai jokingly told me that I posed a danger to him. I enquired how that was so. He said that I had received more ovation from the audience than and with over several lakhs Nepalese serving in the Indian Army and retired personnel with their families in Nepal, I would be a formidable force if I chose to contest elections there. I replied that to do so, I would have to be given Nepalese citizenship, which I was sure he would not give me. The US Ambassador told me that I had an unfair advantage over the other Ambassadors because of my Nepal connection and fluency in Nepali. I was happy to receive compliments from both the Chinese and the Pakistani Ambassadors.

In December 1990, VP Singh Government fell. I felt that I had achieved my main task in Nepal. A new constitution was being drafted in Nepal. I had arranged for an Indian constitutional expert, Shri Singhvi, to be an Adviser. Being a political appointee, I felt that in keeping with democratic traditions, scrupulously observed in the US, I should tender my resignation. Bhattarai tried to persuade me a lot to withdraw my resignation and he also tried to persuade Chandra Shekhar the new Prime Minister of India not to accept my resignation. Neither I withdrew my resignation nor did Chandra Shekhar decline to accept it.

My departure from Nepal was an emotional event. Breaking protocol, the King and Queen came on a farewell visit to my residence and spent an evening with me and my wife. The Nepal Government asked me to give a farewell address to the people of Nepal on the television. The Prime Minister and all members of his Cabinet came to the Embassy to bid me farewell. Bhattarai wrote, "We will always remember General Sinha. He is a true friend of Nepal. He was as much India's Ambassador to Nepal as Nepal's Ambassador to India". VP Singh who was then no longer Prime Minister, stated that General Sinha was our mainstay in Nepal and contributed immensely to improved Indo-Nepal relations.

7

INDEPENDENCE: PARTITION AND ARMY

Army's contribution to India's Independence and its role during the Partition of Sub-Continent, have not received much attention. As one who served in the Army before and after Independence, as also witnessed the Partition holocaust, I would like to place on record my personal recollections of that period.

I joined the British Indian Army during the Second World War and continued serving in the Army of Independent India. Having served in Burma (now Myanmar) and Netherlands East Indies (now Indonesia), I returned home to India and landed in Calcutta (now Kolkata). I was in an army transit camp on 16 August 1946 when Jinnah launched his Direct Action Day. The Muslim League Premier of Bengal, Suhrawardy faithfully carried out the genocide in which thousands got killed in Kolkata, followed by killings and abductions in Noakhali. The calling out of the Army in Kolkata was deliberately delayed by Suhrawardy to allow the hoodlums to carry out their mayhem. I witnessed the streets of Kolkata strewn with mutilated dead bodies. Violence in the city abated after the Army was deployed to restore order. A couple of weeks later, I was posted to the Military Operatios Directorate of General Headquarters (now Army Headquarters) at Delhi. This Directorate had hitherto been an exclusive British preserve. All the officers and clerks were British. I joined the Directorate in September 1946 along with two other Indian officers, Lt Col (later Field Marshal) Manekshaw and Major Yahya Khan, later President of Pakistan. We were allocated to three different sections of the Directorate: Manekshaw to Planning, Yahya to Frontier Defence and I to Internal Security. At that time, as part of internal security duties, Army was fully preoccupied in combating unprecedented communal violence. Never had the Army been used so extensively in this role. From my perch at Delhi, I got a grandstand view of the cycle of communal violence taking place in the country. Kolkata-Noakhali killings were followed by mass killings of Muslims in Bihar and Garhmukteshwar. The Unionist Ministry then in power in Punjab and the Congress Ministry in NWFP had managed to keep their provinces free of large scale communal violence. In March 1947 a Muslim League Ministry came to power in Punjab and a little later also in NWFP. The floodgates of communal violence of the worst type now raged all over North India. Muslims and non-Muslims (Sikhs and Hindus) were matched evenly in Punjab. Both sides perpetrated the worst type of savagery. The entire population of the region appeared to have gone beserk. Towards the end of July, it was decided to have a Punjab Boundary Force of 50,000 soldiers comprising equal number of units earmarked for India and Pakistan. Major General Pat Rees took over as the commander of this Force. Two Indian Brigadiers, one Hindu remaining in India and the other Muslim going to Pakistan, were appointed his deputies. This experiment did not succeed. Within a month, the Punjab Boundary Force had to be disbanded. The two Dominions took over responsibility for maintaining order in their respective territories. On our side, a new skeleton Command Headquarters, called Delhi and East Punjab Command, was set up with Lt Gen Sir Dudley Russell as the Army Commander. There were some twelve officers on his staff, all of them British except me. I was then a Major dealing with operations. There were three subordinate formations under the Command – Delhi Area under Major General Rajendra Sinhji who later became Army Chief, East Punjab Area under Major General KS Thimayya who also later became Army Chief and Military Evacuation Organisation at Lahore under Major General Chimni. No passenger or goods train except the frontier mail new Golden Temple was running anywhere in Punjab. All the railway rolling stock had been mobilized for carrying refugees. Lakhs of Muslims from all over the country had concentrated in Delhi at three major locations, Purana Qila, Nizamuddin and the open space around the Red Fort. They were being evacuated to Pakistan in refugee trains, escorted by the Army. Hindu and Sikh refugees coming from Pakistan were initially accommodated in a tented refugee camp at Kurukshetra, before being dispersed to other locations. At one time this camp held 5 lakh refugees. There were also long refugee foot columns, several miles long, moving from either side. It was impossible to provide adequate protection to these columns, extending several miles. Air drops of food packages were organized for these columns. The civil administration had collapsed in Punjab and our Command was assigned the duty of restoring order and evacuation of refugees. Mountbatten had made the luxurious Viceroy's special train available to our Command. Russell established his mobile headquarters in that train. We were completely self-contained in the corridor train with accommodation for officers, clerical staff, security personnel and our offices. Our messes and kitchen functioned in the train. We had line and wireless communications on the train as also our motor transport. I operated from this train for nearly two months travelling between Delhi and Lahore. I have in all humility recorded all these details so that some credence may be given to my views on the events of that time based on my personal experience.

As for the Army's contribution towards the Independence of India, one has to go back to the Great Uprising of 1857. The British call it the Sepoy Mutiny or the Great Mutiny and Indian nationalists refer to it as the First War of Indian Independence. Call it what one may, it was primarily an uprising of the Indian soldiers against foreign rule. It lit the spark of nationalism in the country and was a source of great inspiration for succeeding generations in our freedom struggle. The gallantry of the Indian soldiers in battles, during the First World War won world wide acclaim. This was a source of national pride for the Indian people giving them increased self confidence. The emergence of the Indian National Army under Netaji Subhas Chandra Bose during the Second World War, added a new dimension to our freedom struggle. The INA comprised soldiers of the Indian Army taken prisoners by the Japanese in Malaya. The INA trials generated a tremendous patriotic surge all over the country. They were a big shot in the arm for our freedom struggle. This was followed by the Naval Mutiny in Mumbai and Karachi, Army mutiny in Jabalpur and Air Force mutiny in Karachi. This violently shook the foundations of the British Empire in India. It was at this stage and soon after the Great Kolkata killings that I had joined the Military Operations Directorate in Delhi. There were three things that I found both interesting and revealing. First, a plan for the evacuation of all British civilians in India to the UK called Operation Gondola. Second, the operational map that I was required to maintain in the Operations Room. Third, a paper on the reliability of the Indian Army prepared by Major General O'Brien, the Director of Military Intelligence.

The British feared an uprising on the lines of what had happened in 1857. Many British civilians were scattered in different parts of the country. Gondola catered for their initial evacuation to temporary camps in the provinces, at provincial capitals and some selected convenient locations. These were called Keeps. Armed protection with necessary logistic support was to be provided at the Keeps. In the subsequent phase, they were to be evacuated to Safes near the port towns of Kolkata, Vaishakapatnam, Chennai, Cochin, Mumbai and Karachi, awaiting repatriation to the UK. The troops guarding the Safes and Keeps were to be a mix of British and Indian soldiers. In the event, as communal violence escalated, there was no need to implement Plan Gondola. There was now much bitterness and violence between Hindus and Muslims and hardly any against the British. It was a great irony that at the height of the communal carnage in Punjab, British officers could move around unarmed in Delhi and Punjab while Indian officers, whether Muslims or non-Muslims, had to carry arms and in remote areas move with escort.

I had to maintain a large map of India with pins of different colours showing locations of all combat units in the country. Red was for British units, Green for Gorkha units and Brown for Indian units. A distinction was made between Indian and Gorkha units. At that time, the Gorkhas were officered exclusively by the British with no Indian officers in those units. The Indian units had a mix of British and Indian officers with Commanding Officers and senior officers mostly British. The "mutiny syndrome" prevailed among the British. It was ensured that no location had only brown pins without some red and green pins in situ. Field Marshal Auchinleck, the then Commander-in-Chief frequently visited the Operations Room and would study the map maintained by me.

The paper written by the Director Military Intelligence had a novel security classification – Top Secret Not For Indian Eyes. My predecessor, a British officer in a hurry to go back home to the UK for demobilization, had handed over to me the key of almirah containing classified documents without any check of the documents. This paper was written in the wake of INA trials. It stated that the Indian officers of the Army could be divided into three categories – those commissioned before 1933 from Sandhurst, the pre-war officers commissioned between 1933 and 1939 and the wartime emergency commissioned officers. The Sandhurst officers were considered more reliable. They were now middle aged with family commitments and did not nurture much grievance as they had been treated well. They were very few, their total number being about thirty. The pre-war, 1933 to 1939 officers had a grievance because their emoluments were initially not at par with their British counterparts. This disparity was removed during the war but its memory and of other discriminations still rankled with them. They numbered about 500. The wartime officers numbering about 12,000 were considered very unreliable. While in their schools and colleges, they had been exposed to subversive political influence culminating in the Quit India movement. They faced an uncertain future because they were all emergency commissioned officers and only very few were likely to be absorbed in the permanent post-war cadre of the Army. They were working at the company and platoon level interacting directly with the soldiers. As for the soldiers, position regarding them had also changed radically. Prior to war, strength of the Army was 1.37 lakhs and recruitment was confined to the martial classes. A large number of soldiers came from traditional military families. During the war, floodgates had been opened for recruitment. The Army had been expanded from 1.37 lakhs to 2.2 millions. The INA had had a psychological impact on the officers and men of the Army. Further, the bulk of Army overseas had served in South East Asia, where they had seen how the prestige of the White Man in the early years of the war had suffered at the hands of the Japanese. Towards the end of war, national movements for freedom had erupted in Asian countries, ruled by colonial powers like the British, the French, the Dutch and the Portugese. The paper also took into account the surmise that an economically exhausted Britain after a long drawn out war, was not in a position to maintain a strong British military presence in India. In the circumstance, the paper recommended early British withdrawal from India. I was much impressed by this very analytical study. The fact that Indian Army had an impact on our movement for Independence and hastened the dawn of freedom, is indisputable. Earl Atlee the British Prime Minister, who had presided over the liquidation of the British Empire in 1947, confirmed this during his visit to India in 1956. He told Mr Chakravarty, then Governor of Bengal, that decision to quit quickly in 1947 had been taken because the British could no longer rely on the loyalty of Indian Army.

The role of the Army during Partition has not so far been factored into discussions about Partition. The fact that the Army also influenced the decision on Partition, needs to be taken into account. After their experience with Cromwell's military dictatorship, the British ardently nurtured the concept of an apolitical army. It suited them to transplant that concept in the Indian Army that they raised. While this concept continues to hold good in India, it got thrown overboard in Pakistan for reasons which we need not discuss here. After 1857, the British decided not to have one class regiment except for Gorkhas and Garhwalis. All other combat units of the Indian Army had the composition of 50% Muslims and 50% non-Muslims (Hindus and Sikhs). This was in line with their policy of Divide and Rule. Different communities living together in war and peace and encouraged to remain apolitical, developed a regimental ethos which held them together. I was commissioned in the Jat Regiment which had two companies of Jat Hindus and two companies of Muslims. I served with a Punjabi Muslim company. I found that the regimental spirit among the men was strong and there was no communal divide. This continued in the Army as a whole till the end of 1946 but started cracking in 1947; reaching a breaking point by August 1947. Yet I saw that when the Muslim companies of the Jat Regiment were going to Pakistan, tears were shed on both sides. This happened in other regiments as well.

In keeping with the Army's apolitical traditions, Indian officers during the British days, hardly ever discussed political matters among themselves. I recall that in Rangoon soon after the end of the war, one junior British officer referred to the INA as traitors and also used vulgar epithets for it. There was no senior officer present in the Mess. This led to a heated discussion between the British and Indian officers, both Hindus and Muslims. Although politics in India had got much communalized in the Forties, Netaji seems to have promoted complete communal harmony in the Azad Hind Government and the Indian National Army. Vande Matram as an anthem had been a source of discord between the two communities in India. Netaji had coined the slogan Jai Hind which could not raise any communal hackles.

The Indian Army got involved in a strange war in Indonesia. It had been sent to that country primarily to take the surrender of the Japanese. The Dutch had been driven out from those islands. They accompanied the Indian Army to re-establish their colonial rule. The Indonesians had declared their Independence and had raised an army of their own. The Indian Army got involved in fighting the Indonesians. It was a strange situation for us. The Indonesians would tell us that we were ourselves not free and yet we were fighting against their becoming independent. During my service in Indonesia, I used to feel very embarrassed on this account. However, what surprised me was that when the Indonesians raised the banner of Islam in their appeal to Indian soldiers, a number of Muslim soldiers of the Indian Army deserted and joined them. I was told that about a thousand or more of our Muslim soldiers had deserted. They got left behind when we came out from Indonesia. I am mentioning this because this was for the first time that I saw the communal virus affecting the Army.

Notwithstanding the early signs in Indonesia, it is remarkable that during the outbreak of unprecedented communal violence in August 1946 and till well after 1947 had set in, the Indian soldier, both Hindu and Muslim, showed complete impartiality when called upon to deal with communal violence. This was so in Kolkata in August 1946, in Bihar in October 1946 and in Garhmukteshwar (U.P.) in November 1946. Two or three battalions of the Bihar Regiment which had Hindus and Muslims in equal number, had operated in Bihar during the communal riots and had remained completely impartial. The Bihar riots were horrendous. For the first time communal riots had spread so extensively to rural areas. Hitherto communal riots had remained an urban phenomenon. Several thousand Muslims got massacred in Bihar as a revenge for thousands of Hindus killed in Kolkata and Noakhali. At the time of Bihar riots, I was in Delhi getting daily reports of what was happening in my home province. Colonel Naser Ali Khan, who later went to Pakistan Army and I were serving at General Headquarters and were living in the officers mess on Wellesley Road (now Zakir Hussain Road). He was many years senior to me and was always very kind to me. One morning at breakfast after having read a report about Bihar riots in the newspaper, he told me excitedly that his blood boiled when he remembered that I was a Bihari. I told him that I condemned what was happening in Bihar more than him. He was not the only Muslim officer I interacted with in Delhi, who felt so worked up over the most unfortunate happenings in Bihar. I am mentioning these incidents to bring out how circumstances were forcing communal virus to spread in the Army. Till March 1947 things appeared to be well under control. Communal riots were taking place in different places and the Army deployed to maintain order remained very disciplined and impartial. Wavell during his farewell address on 21 March 1947, said, "I believe that the stability of the Indian Army may perhaps be the deciding factor in the future of India". Pakistan had not emerged as a sovereign State till then and hardly anyone could imagine that it will become a reality in the next four months.

With Muslim League Ministries coming to power both in Punjab and NWFP, communal passions were sought to be aroused in a planned manner. Pictures of atrocities on Muslims in Bihar and Garhmukteshwar started being shown in mosques along with fiery speeches by Muslim clerics on Fridays. Widespread communal riots erupted in Peshawar and Rawalpindi. Soon the whole of North India was in flames. The strain started showing on soldiers. Most of the soldiers, both Muslims and non-Muslims, were from the North. Their homeland was getting ravaged and in several cases their families had been victims of communal frenzy. It was becoming increasingly difficult for the soldiers to retain their impartiality. The downslide in this regard became more perceptible after Partition was announced. The day after that announcement I met two officers in their uniforms in Delhi wearing strange shoulder tittles – RPE and RPASC. In those days officers from Engineers and Army Service Corps wore shoulder titles, RIE for Royal Indian Engineers and RIASC for Royal Indian Army Service Corps. Some officers had begun to wear Pakistan shoulder titles within hours of the Partition announcement and much before Pakistan came into being. There were reports of senior Muslim officers going to meet Jinnah who then lived in his house at 10 Aurangzeb Road. This showed how officers going to Pakistan were getting politicized. It also showed the fervour for Pakistan among some Muslim officers. On the morrow of Independence in August 1947, the Gilgit Scouts staged a coup arresting Brigadier Ghansara Singh of Kashmir Army, who had been sent there as Governor by Maharaja. This was the first military coup in Pakistan. More were to follow later.

As mentioned earlier, the Punjab Boundary Force comprising in equal measure, units earmarked for Indian and Pakistan Army, was set up under a British commander in July 1947. It was hoped that it will help in maintaining order on both sides of the border, at a time when communal violence and migration had reached a crescendo. The experiment failed because the impartiality of the soldier had got eroded and there were several instances of soldiers taking sides. Large scale violence again erupted in Kolkata and Mahatma Gandhi had gone there to restore sanity among the people. He undertook a fast which had a dramatic effect. It was then that Mountbatten made his famous remark that a one man boundary force had succeeded in Kolkata while the 50,000 strong Punjab Boundary Force had failed in the North. The Punjab Boundary Force was disbanded within six weeks of its raising and the two Dominions assumed responsibility for maintaining order on their side of the border.

As a tailpiece, I may add that after a couple of months, Indian and Pakistan Armies were locked in fighting a war against each other in Kashmir.

No doubt the Partition holocaust was the greatest tragedy in the history of the Sub Continent in which millions were killed and millions were uprooted. Soon after Hindus and Muslims had fought unison in the First War of Independence in 1857, the seeds of separatism were sown by Sir Syed Ahmed. He conceived a separate nationhood for the Muslims of India. Lord Morley by accepting separate electorate in 1906 provided oxygen for it. This became a raging storm and was exploited to the hilt by Jinnah. Looking back in hindsight, one can say that Partition could have been averted had the Congress been more accommodative and the Muslim League less obdurate. However, after the planned genocide started by Jinnah on 16 August 1946 as part of his Direct Action programme, there could be no going back from the path of disaster. The Qaid-e-Azam had become Qatl-e- Azam. The puerile attempt by some people to underscore Jinnah's secular image on the basis of a lone speech by him while inaugurating the Pakistan Constituent Assembly does not carry conviction. One swallow does not make a summer. It now transpires that Jinnah made that conciliatory address not out of any goodwill but under compulsion. The inside story has been revealed in a book Select Documents on Partition of India by a distinguished historian, Dr Kripal Singh. Lord Ismay the Chief of Staff of Lord Mountbatten told him in an interview on August 17, 1964, the background to that much hailed address. Mountbatten had asked Ismay to convey to Jinnah the need for his taking that line, now that he had achieved his Pakistan. The sole aim was to check the spiraling violence in Pakistan and the counter violence in East Punjab. That Jinnah's animosity towards India had not changed, is made amply clear by Pakistan's invasion of Kashmir launched on 22 October 1947. His earlier slogan was India Divided or India Destroyed. That had now changed to India Divided and India Destroyed. It is a different matter that on 7 November 1947 the Indian Army turned back that invasion from the outskirts of Srinagar. This was perhaps in line with what Charles Martel had achieved at Tours in 732 against the Saracens thereby saving France or Jan Sobleski had done in 1683, throwing back the Turks from the gates of Vienna and saved Europe.

Lately attempts have been made by some people to exonerate Jinnah for his role in Partition. They have even gone further, by trying to blame Patel and Nehru for accepting Partition. It is even insinuated that they were tired and old, and were in a hurry to grab power. Having opposed the two nation theory and partition all their lives, they caved in and opted for Partition. Ralph Emerson rightly wrote, "A foolish consistency is the hobgoblin of little minds". In Army the saying is: consistency is the hallmark of a mule. Sardar Patel had the uncanny gift of foresight and the ability to take hard decisions. He rightly assessed the situation prevailing in mid 1947. Based on his experience in the Interim Government when the Muslim League had brought government functioning to a grinding halt, the crescendo of communal violence and the Army getting contaminated combating communal violence for nearly a year; he realized that there was now no alternative to Partition. His decision to salvage the wreck in 1947 was an act of great statesmanship. If that had not been done, things would have become much worse. We would have had a civil war on our hands with the Army broken up and participating from both sides. One does not know what the outcome of such a conflict may have been. Had a patchwork solution of unity with a weak centre been accepted in 1947, the results could have been disastrous. With a weak Centre, the integration of the 500 odd Princely States may not have been possible. The minority population of India was about 12% in 1947. Today, the combined minority population in an undivided India would have been 40%. Petrol funded Islamist forces that have now emerged in the world, would have swamped India. India as we know it today, would not have existed. Patel's coming to terms with a moth eaten Pakistan and getting the Congress to accept it, was a great achievement. This was almost at par with his universally hailed achievement of integrating the Princely States with the Indian Union.

The first vivisection of India had taken place in the beginning of the second millennium. Although the Arabs had conquered Sindh in 712 AD, they had remained confined to the deserts of Sindh for three centuries during which Afghanistan had remained part of India. During this period, the Hindu Shahi dynasty ruled over Afghanistan from Kabul. They guarded the country's North West Frontier. Starting from 999 AD, they succumbed to repeated invasions of the great conqueror and plunderer, Mahmud Gazni. India was exposed for the first time to the ferocity of religious fundamentalism. Soon, Afghanistan ceased to be a part of India. That was our country's first vivisection. The second took place in 1947 again on account of religious fundamentalism. Sardar Patel ensured that the 80% residual India was fully integrated and became a strong nation. Despite that part of the country which broke away becoming a theocracy and carrying out instant ethnic cleansing in the West and gradual in the East, Nehru and Patel ensured that India retained her secular values.

In August 1947 the residual Muslim League in India adopted a resolution reviving itself. Surprisingly, undeterred with all that had happened leading to Partition, its representatives in the Constituent Assembly, demanded reservation for Muslims and also separate electorate. Muslim members of the Assembly other than the few of the Muslim League, did not support this demand. It got rejected by an overwhelming majority. Speaking on this issue the Sardar stated, "I know they have a mandate from the Muslim League to move this amendment. I feel sorry for them. This is not a place for acting on madness. This is a place today to act on your conscience and to act for the good of the country. For a community to think that its interests are different from that of the country in which it lives, is a great mistake". Unfortunately the successors of Sardar Patel in his party have shown lack of vision. For the sake of garnering Muslim votes, they have been following the policy of appeasement and are prepared in that process to sacrifice national interest. BK Nehru, an eminent member of the dynasty, in his autobiography, Nice Guys Finish Second, wrote that the old guard in the Congress considered national interests supreme but the new generation feels otherwise, giving priority to party interests. The Congress practicing secularism selectively has been giving an impetus to communalism. It treats Muslim League as a secular party and welcomes it as an alliance partner in the Government, both at the Centre and in Kerala. It treats the BJP as untouchable and wants to have nothing to do with it, even when BJP has Muslim members but

Muslim League does not have a single non-Muslim member. It has been facilitating the illegal migration of Bangladeshi Muslims to build its vote bank. A Congress Prime Minister declares that Muslims must have the first call on the Nation's resources. It has been decided to set up four new Muslim Universities like the Aligarh Muslim University, which had been the nursery for Pakistan. Several other such instances can be quoted. If we continue like this, the day is not far when we will have to put up with a third vivisection of the country. The second partition was the product of separate electorate, the third may be the product of the policy of appeasement. Justice in full measure must be provided to the minority but appeasement can be disastrous both for them and the country.

The Indian Army made a significant contribution towards ushering the independence of India. Its role during the Partition holocaust was also of great significance. And today, the Army has been combating secessionist forces including the Jihadis in Kashmir. I conclude quoting from Stephen Cohen's book on the Indian Army. "India has virtually ignored the military as a factor in nation building. This is surprising, for the military had a profound impact on the course of nationalist politics and also upon policies after 1947."

PART-II
NATIONAL SECURITY

8

NATIONAL SECURITY, STRATEGY, STRUCTURE: THE WAY AHEAD

Walter Lipman's definition of national security is very apt. He wrote that a nation has security when it does not have to sacrifice its legitimate interests to avoid war and is able when challenged to uphold them by war. Our earnest desire as a nation has been to develop a prosperous, peaceful and secular democracy and gain our due place in the comity of nations. We have no territorial ambitions and want to live in peace with our neighbours and the rest of the world. Yet since Independence, we have had to defend our country, in wars repeatedly thrust upon us by our neighbours.

National security implies the ability of a nation to preserve and protect its chosen way of life. The way of life we have chosen for ourselves is fundamentally different from our two powerful nuclear armed neighbours, with whom we have territorial disputes. One believes in theocracy and religious fundamentalism as against secularism chosen by us. The other has chosen dictatorship of the proletariat and one party rule as opposed to our faith in the freedom of the individual and a multi-party polity. These two neighbours have formed a nexus against us.

In globalised world, a nation has to view its security in the context of the prevailing world order. At the time of our Independence and for forty years thereafter, we lived in the era of Cold War, when the two Super Powers neutralized each other. In 1971 Nixon sent the US aircraft carrier Enterprise to the Bay of Bengal to threaten India. This threat got neutralized by Soviet submarines shadowing the American warship. Today things have changed and we live in a unipolar world with the USA as the lone Super Power. The USA and India being secular democracies, should be natural allies. Of late, there has been much talk of strategic consensus between them. This has been underscored by recently concluded, the Indo-US nuclear deal. Yet more things seem to have changed, the more they remain the same. In the past, Pakistan freely used US weapons given to it for operations against the Soviet, in wars against India. The US turned a blind eye to this. Even the burning of its US embassy in Islamabad was forgiven by the USA for Pakistan's support during the Cold War. Despite all the tall talk of nuclear proliferation, USA ignored transfer of nuclear weapon technology and delivery system by China to Pakistan and all the assistance provided to Pakistan to become a nuclear weapon power. AQ Khan's nuclear deals with North Korea, Iran and Libya too were overlooked. Today, Pakistan is an indispensible US ally in the war against Islamist terrorism. US military and economic aid running into several billions US dollars are being poured into Pakistan. No less a person than General Musharraf, former President of Pakistan has openly asserted that weapons received for terror war from the US, have been diverted for use against India. As in the past, a US has again turned a blind eye to this. Strong Anti-American feelings prevailing among the people of Pakistan, is also being ignored. Fanatics in that country have been vociferous in asserting that the US is their enemy number one. Notwithstanding all this, Pakistan continues to be the most favoured non-NATO ally of US. India must accept that despite all the talk of friendly relations with US, the latter's tilt towards Pakistan will continue. This aspect needs to be factored into our national security plans.

The impact of our neighbouring countries on our national security has to be highlighted. China is our big neighbour in the North, with whom we share a 4000 mile long border. Prior to 1947, the British Empire extending from Aden to Singapore was all powerful, South of the Himalayas. In the North, China was a splintered country with warring warlords. After the demise of British Empire, there are now four sovereign States, South of the Himalayas, each following an independent policy after the Communist Revolution, a monolithic power has emerged North of the Himalayas which today is on the fast track to become a Super Power. The pendulum of power has swung very much to the North of the Himalayas. In 1962 we suffered a humiliating defeat at the hands of Chinese due to our unpreparedness and the failure of our underscored political decision and mustered supermercy over the military leadership. The 1967 artillery duel in Sikkim to an extent restored our prestige. After the famous Mao smile of the Seventies, relations between the two countries improved and diplomatic relations were restored. Dialogue to resolve the border dispute has continued for the last eighteen years. It has been proceeding at an excruciatingly slow pace. However, tranquility has been maintained on the border and no firing incidents have taken place. China's policy appears to be to keep the borders with India tranquil but not solve the dispute; trade with India but arm Pakistan. After Vajpayee's historic visit to China in 2003, a marked improvement took place in Sino-Indian relations. China gave up its previous stand of Sikkim not being a part of India. It now recognized Sikkim as a State of India. Nathu La was opened for trade. This trade has shot up to 18 million US dollars and after Hu Jintao's visit, it was agreed to raise it to 40 million US dollars by 2010. Importantly, during Vajpayee's visit, it was also agreed that while delineating the border, settled population on either side will not be disturbed. This implied that Tawang's position would not be disturbed. Despite these positive developments, China has continued with its policy of keeping India strategically locked in South Asia. It has a string of pearls encircling India. It has established naval bases at Coco Islands in Myanmar, at Hambantola in Sri Lanka and at Gawadar in Pakistan. It has also been trying to bring Nepal, Myanmar, Bangladesh and Sri Lanka in its area of influence. It has been arming Pakistan with both conventional and nuclear weapons. With its encirclement policy, China is trying to chain India like a lion in a cage. Simultaneously, China has been building up its military capability in Tibet at a tremendous pace. A railway line and an oil pipeline have been constructed from

Gormo to Lhasa. The former is being extended to Tibet-Nepal border. A super East-West highway has been constructed in Tibet. Operational airfields, missile bases, and logistic dumps have been developed. China now has the capability to maintain 24 divisions in Tibet and concentrate such a large force there in two to three weeks. Yet another matter of concern is the fact of China diverting the Brahmaputra to feed its arid region in the North and produce 40,000 MW of electricity. That will render India's North East region dry. That will be catastrophic for us. This may appear a little far fetched but its possibility cannot be ignored nor can one overlook the adverse ecological impact of this on the entire region. Since 2007 there has been a downslide in Sino-Indian relations. China has raised the pitch of its rhetoric on Arunachal Pradesh and tried to block Asian Development Bank loan to India. Its opposition to India's permanent membership of UN Security Council continues. A think tank in China has come out with an idea that China should bring about the disintegration of India breaking it into several States. There has also been an increase in border incursions which has received much publicity in the Indian media. The Government has been trying to play this down saying that it is not something abnormal and the border remains tranquil.

Let us now discuss the threat we face from Pakistan. The origin and history of Pakistan is one of relentless hostility towards India. The refusal to accept to live in a country with Hindu majority led to the creation of Pakistan. Today, they find it difficult to digest that India has progressed more than them and is set to become a great power in the not too distant future. We gave Pakistan, the most favoured nation (MFN) status for trade long ago. That has not yet been reciprocated by them. Pakistanis misread history and fancy themselves as the descendents of Central Asian conquerors who on several occasions, successfully invaded India in the medieval period. The fact, however, is that they are the descendents of the indigenous people who converted to Islam. Their romanticized view of their martial superiority received a setback in 1947, a big jolt in 1965 and got shattered in 1971. There was now an overpowering urge to avenge the defeat of 1971. Zulfikar Ali Bhutto talked of one thousand years war with India. Having found it difficult to defeat India in conventional war, Zia-ul-

Haq crafted the strategy of thousand cuts to bleed India to death in Kashmir. This also has not yielded the desired result. Pakistan has now extended Jehadi terrorism to the Indian mainland. The terror attack in Mumbai on 26/11 in 2008 was the mother of such attacks. Hafeez Mohammad Sayeed the master mind behind 26/11 had spoken on November 3, 2000, "Jihad is not about Kashmir only. Fifteen years ago people would have found it ridiculous if someone had told them about the disintegration of the Soviet Union. Insha Allah, today I announce the break up of India. We will not rest till the whole of India is dissolved into Pakistan". His followers wildly cheered him and announced that they would soon unfurl their green flag on Red Fort. Not long after this speech, his followers launched a terrorist attack at Red Fort and attacked our symbols of democracy. They targeted first the Jammu and Kashmir Assembly and then the Indian Parliament. They have also been repeatedly attacking the country's financial capital at Mumbai. Pakistan has been propagating that Kashmir is the core issue and once that gets resolved, Indo-Pakistan relations will get normalized and become cordial. This is misleading. The fact is that Kashmir is not the cause but the symptom of the disease. It is pertinent that while addressing a meeting at Karachi on 19 April 1999, Musharraf stated that low intensity conflict against India will continue even after the Kashmir issue was resolved. Pakistan is the epi-centre of international terrorism. There is always a Pakistan connection in any major act of Islamist terrorism anywhere in the world. Of late, Pakistan has been hoist on its own petard. It is also a victim of Islamist terrorism and its people have been suffering numerous terrorist attacks. Despite its record of a rogue State and of a nuclear proliferator, Pakistan has been the beneficiary of American benevolence which has kept it going. This has been because Pakistan has served America's interest during the cold war, in the war against the Soviets in Afghanistan and now in the war against Islamists terrorism. It has also been receiving generous military and economic support from China because of its utility in keeping India in check. Pakistan is known to violate written agreements which it has been signing. It violated the Cease Fire agreement by launching the 1965 war, the Tashkent agreement by initiating the 1971 war, the Shimla accord by starting a proxy war in Kashmir and the Lahore declaration by the intrusion in Kargil. It has also been repeatedly contradicting its own stand. In 1947 it stated that it was not involved in the tribal invasion of Kashmir but in 1948 it admitted its involvement. Major General Akbar Khan, the commander of that invading force wrote a book Raiders over Kashmir, giving details of Pakistan complicity and involvement. In 1965 again, Pakistan denied any hand in starting the war saying that it was an uprising of the people of Kashmir. General Moosa, the C-in-C of Pakistan Army in that war, wrote a book My Version, in which he revealed how that war was started by Pakistan. It was the same story with the Kargil war. As for terrorism in Kashmir, Pakistan had always been denying its involvement saying that it was a freedom struggle of the people of Kashmir for which it was providing only moral support. And now President Zardari has admitted that Pakistan had been using terrorism as State policy, There was the same perfidy again over the nationality of Kasab captured during the Mumbai terror attack and Pakistan involvement in that horrendous incident.

Our other neighbours are Afghanistan, Nepal, Bhutan, Bangladesh and Myanmar. Afghanistan used to have a friendly attitude towards India before the Soviet invasion of that country and it did not have cordial relations with Pakistan. I remember when as Director Military Intelligence, I visited Kabul after the 1971 war, Afghan Army Chief told me that India and Afghanistan should have had an alliance during the 1971 war. In that event Indian and Afghan Armies could have shaken hands across the Indus. It is a pity that our Defence planners have had to work on two front strategy against China and Pakistan but we never forced a two front strategy on Pakistan. After the Soviet invasion of Afghanistan and Talibanisation in that country, things have changed drastically. Today India is giving development and humanitarian aid to the people of Afghanistan but this is resented by Pakistan and the Taliban. US military commanders, in Afghanistan do not seem to be comfortable with this.

Nepal's cultural, economic and historical links with India are very deep rooted. The two countries have an open border. About a million Nepalese are employed in various jobs in India with about 70,000 in the Indian Army. Fortyfive per cent of the population of Nepal is of Indian origin. There is political instability in Nepal. Maoists with their leanings towards China are trying to gain ascendancy in Nepal. This poses a threat to the Gangetic Valley from Hardwar to Kolkata, the heartland of India.

Bhutan has been the most friendly neighbour of India which has always stood by us at every international fora. Democracy with constitutional monarchy has recently been introduced in Bhutan.

Bangladesh came into being largely with the help and sacrifice of Indian forces. After the assassination of Bangabandhu, politics took a different turn with growing anti India feelings. Secularism lost ground. Islamists became very powerful and the Bangladesh adopted an anti-India stance. Unabated illegal migration from Bangladesh has been posing both security and demographic problems for India. Indian militants have found shelter in Bangladesh. The recent overwhelming electoral victory of Sheikh Hasina and her coming to power holds out hope for secularism in Bangladesh and for good Indo-Bangladesh relations.

Myanmar has been under the rule of a military junta for a long time. Our sympathy has been with Aung Su Kyi, the democratically elected leader who has been held in prison for many years. This has come in the way of our developing close relations with the Myanmar Government. China has been gaining increasing influence in that country. It has economic and military ties with Myanmar.

Our neighbor in the South, is Sri Lanka. Our relations with Sri Lankan Government have been cordial although we have been hamstrung by the conflicting pulls of political parties in Tamil Nadu. Sri Lanka has just emerged from a long period of insurgency. The LTTE has been wiped out and things have started looking up in Sri Lanka. There is need for Sri Lankan Government to work out a political solution acceptable to the Tamils of that country and at the same time maintaining the country's integrity.

Terrorism constitutes the biggest internal threat to our national security. We have to contend with all the three types of terrorism – secessionist, religious and revolutionary. Secessionist terrorism erupted first in the North East. It started in Nagaland and then spread to Mizoram, Manipur and Tripura. These were basically tribal insurgencies. Culturally and historically the tribes had not been assimilated with the rest of India. The population of these areas is sparse and this region is confined to fringe areas on our border. Naga militancy has been dormant for last thirteen years with cease fire holding. Hopefully, a political settlement will emerge in due course. Over two decades ago, militancy came to an end through a political settlement. Today Mizoram is the most peaceful State of the North East. The violence in Tripura is more in the nature of ethnic conflict between the tribal population and the immigrants from erstwhile East Pakistan in the wake of Partition. The original inhabitants have been reduced to a minority. The ongoing militancy in Manipur is a matter of concern. The ULFA militancy in the Brahmaputra Valley of Assam is the most serious of all the threats in North East. Population of Assam is more than double the total population of remaining six States of North East. Economically, Assam with its oil and tea wealth, is better off than other States of the region. Abutting on the narrow Siliguri corridor, Assam provides India the only land link to the entire North East land mass. I was Governor of Assam for six years. When I assumed my appointment in 1997, militancy was at its peak in the State. We managed to turn round the situation through a three pronged strategy of co-ordinated and intensive operations, economic development and psychological initiatives. Military operations broke the back of ULFA militancy. The Bhutanese Army cleared ULFA camps in Bhutan. As part of economic development, we installed one lakh shallow tube wells in Assam turning it from a rice deficit to a rice surplus State. The influx of illegal migrants from Bangladesh had been the root cause for start of insurgency in the State. I took up this issue through a 42 page printed report to the President. This had a very healthy impact among the Assamese people. We projected the three icons of Assam, Mahapurush Shankardev, Lachchit Borphukan and Lokpriya Gopinath Bordoloi as national heroes through various measures. I repeatedly declared that my aim was to make the people of Assam proud of their past and the rest of India proud of Assam. The cumulative effect of all this was spectacular. Previously when, an ULFA militant was killed, he was hailed as a hero and there would be funeral orations praising him. All that ceased. Over a period of time, 81 militants were apprehended by villagers in rural areas, half of whom were lynched and the other half handed over to the Police. Surrenders of ULFA militants to Security Forces now started being watched appreciatively by large numbers of local people. Unfortunately, after I left Assam on account of policy of appeasement, there has been a big slide down and violence has again become rampant in Assam.

Religious fundamentalism has been the basic cause for secessionist movement in Jammu and Kashmir. Militancy in that State has been a mix of terrorism, insurgency and proxy war. It has been an international hotspot for long. I was moved from Assam to Kashmir in 2003 and till 2008, I was the Governor there. We tried out the same three pronged strategy that had worked in Assam. We reduced the level of violence considerably through intensive military operations. Through special economic package we tried to woo both the Gujjar Bakherwals and Kashmiri Muslims. We installed one thousand micro hydel projects based on water mills providing electricity to remote villages in mountains. We tried to counter religious fundamentalism through propagating Kashmiriyat, which stands for amity across religious divide. We did not succeed as much as we had done in Assam because religious fundamentalism was too deep rooted and Pakistani involvement too great. On the media front, we failed badly despite our limited efforts. Delhi made no effort to have a vigorous media policy in Kashmir. We found it difficult to eliminate the feeling of alienation among the people. Kashmir continues to be a major festering problem.

Jehadi terrorism with limited support of the people is prevalent in Kashmir. Jehadi terrorist attacks sponsored by Pakistan have been taking place in our mainland cities. The terror attack in Mumbai on 26/11 exposed many chinks in our political and professional armour. As usual, Pakistan first denied complicity and after much flip flop, because of overwhelming evidence, admitted that the attack was launched from its soil by its nationals. However, two years have passed and it has been dragging its feet and not taken action in the matter.

Another type of terrorism of the Left extreme variety, called Naxal terrorism, poses a very serious challenge to our national security. 20 States, 233 districts and 2,000 Police Stations are affected by this menace. Naxal movement is led by the people totally dedicated to the teachings of Marx and Mao. A Red corridor seems to have been established from the borders with Nepal through Bihar, Jharkhand, Orissa, Chhattisgarh and Madhya Pradesh to Andhra Pradesh. The thickly forested area of 7,000 square miles, mostly in Chhattisgarh, comprising 20,000 tribals and 237 villages has become a haven for Naxals. They call this a liberated zone where they run a parallel government administering justice through public courts. Through extortion from businessmen, contractors and even government officials, they manage to raise 500 to 700 crores a year. They have been able to acquire a formidable array of modern weapons and explosives. Their total strength is estimated to be 20,000 underground and 50,000 over ground workers, They have been carrying out spectacular strikes like looting a district police armoury and carrying away 500 rifles, attacking jails to rescue colleagues and release prisoners, attacking railway trains, railway stations, police stations and so on. It is estimated that they are responsible for 80 per cent of violence in the country.

Having examined the different types of threats, namely nuclear war, conventional war and terrorism of all types, we need to broadly discuss the strategy we should adopt. George Tanham was not very wrong when he wrote that India does not have a strategic doctrine. I feel that we carry the dead weight of history. Throughout the medieval period and the early modern era, invaders found us unprepared and we succumbed to invasions. We never sent our armies on expeditions beyond our borders. We suffer from what I call the Panipat syndrome. Even today, our thinking in facing these challenges has always been almost entirely defensive; ignoring the fact that a war can be won primarily by offensive action. Ditch cum bund that has been put up in the West can be a means to an end but not an end in itself.

We face both nuclear and conventional threats from China and Pakistan. China is way ahead of us in both. Our recently retired Naval Chief has stated that we cannot match Chinese military strength. Our Air Force Chief has expressed concern over the fact that our Air Force is one third of the size of the Chinese Air Force. Chinese build up in Tibet and increased border incursions have been much highlighted by the media. No doubt, all this is of much concern but there is no need for any hysteria or panic. 2010 is not 1962. China also has its problems with uprisings in Tibet and all the violence in its Sinkiang province. It is feverishly developing its economic strength wanting to take a lead over the USA in the coming decades and become the leading Super Power of the world. Getting embroiled in a war is not in its national interest. However, we cannot afford to be complacent as we seem to have been for the past many years. China with an economy three times as large as India's, spends 4.3% of its GDP on Defence while India spends less than 3%. For the past many years, 30% of funds allocated for modernization of our Defence Services have remained unutilized due to our archaic and cumbersome procedures for acquiring military hardware. For thirty years we have been trying to acquire self propelled medium artillery and have not yet been able to do so. Our record in regard to tanks, warships and fighter planes is not much better. We need to build up our military strength and improve the infrastructure near our borders. We should not only have strong defensive posture near the border to deter military misadventure but must a develop a military strike capability in Tibet. We need to have a blue water navy to dominate the Indian Ocean. All this can be done while maintaining overt cordial relations with China. We may not be able to match China in military strength but our defence capability must be credible enough to make China realize that she cannot have a military walk over. It may get embroiled in a long drawn war. So far as the string of pearls is concerned, we need to break it by reaching out to Afghanistan, Myanmar, Bangladesh, Viet Nam and Sri Lanka. At the same time ensure that Chinese do not become dominant in Nepal. So far as Pakistan is concerned, we must at all times maintain a marked edge over that rogue State, pathologically hostile to India. We must have plans and capability for offensive action against Pakistan. There is no harm in having dialogue with Pakistan but it should be from a position of strength.

The threat from terrorism can be countered through sound intelligence. The example of British intelligence services thwarting the heinous plans of blowing up trans-Atlantic airliners should be emulated. Sound security arrangements as adopted by the USA against terrorism in its homeland need to be adopted. Plans must also be there to react offensively and take on terrorist bases in case of cross border terrorism. Vote bank politics and the policy of appeasement can be suicidal in dealing with terrorism. Both in the case of secessionist and Naxal terrorism through good governance and development activities, terrorists can be isolated from the people.

I have spelt out threats to our national security and the strategy required to meet those threats. I shall now dwell on organizational structure. A foolproof command and control set up for nuclear forces and a second strike capability are imperative to deter nuclear strike or nuclear blackmail. The Indian higher defence organization is the most irrational in world. Half hearted attempts to improve it after the Kargil war are not enough. We need a Chief of Defence Staff and a fully integrated Ministry of Defence. As for our Police organization, the neglect of police station which is the cutting edge of Police administration is appalling. The present unduly top heavy organization of the Police should be reduced and ranks upgraded at the level of the Police station. It is more important to have more Deputy Superintendent of Police functioning from police stations than having numerous DGs and ADGs Police in States and introducing a new tier of Police functioning in Police Zones above Police Ranges. I have projected my views on the threats to our national security and, strategy and organizational structure that we need.

9

SECESSIONIST MOVEMENTS

The issue of secessionist movement is great concern for all of us at a time when the national security scenario in our country, to put it mildly, is not very encouraging. We need to face the challenges to our national security in a resolute, determined and united manner. Before discussing secessionist movements we face, we must be clear in our mind about what is a nation and to what extent we are a nation in the accepted sense.

My generation grew up at a time when Britain ruled over India. India was then part of an Empire over which the Sun never set. After the First World War, the Empire had past its high noon and after Second World War, the Empire was moving towards sunset. However, the British had been propagating two myths about India. First, they claimed that they united India for the first time under the umbrella of their rule, through their administration, language, railways and telegraph. Second, that Indians were not a nation and if the British quit, India will break into several parts. These myths particularly the first, found many takers among Indians. Even today, the first myth lingers and many in our country believe in it.

The British claim to have united India for the first time flies in the face of history. The Mauryas had done so over two millennia earlier. Their Empire, which included Afghanistan was larger than the British Empire in India. After the Mauryas, political unity of the country was again brought about by Guptas, Delhi Sultans and the Mughal Emperors. The second myth about Indians not being a nation is equally baseless. Churchill said,

"India is a geographical term; it is no more a nation than the Equator". He was wrong. India has been a civilization State from the dawn of history. We need to recall the famous lines of poet Allama Iqbal :

> Yunan Misr-a-Roma sab mit gaen Jahan se,
>
> Ab tak magar hai baqi namo-nishan hamara ;
>
> Kuch bat hai kih hasti mitati nahin hamari,
>
> Sadion raha hai dushman, daure zaman hamara.

A nation is a product of geography, history, culture, civilization and above all a feeling of common identity among its people. The landmass of South Asia encompassed by the mountains in the North, jungles in the East, ocean in the South and desert in the West, has been Bharatvarsh from the time immemorial. The concept of mother country has been deified in India with temples of Bharat Mata. To underscore our common identity, our ancestors chose our pilgrimages in the four corners of our country, Badrinath in the North, Puri in East, Rameshwaram in South and and Dwarka in the West. The Sikh religion which came later in time also promoted a similar concept with their holy places of Naukana, Amritsar, Hemkunt, Patna and Nander in all the four directions within.

With the demise of British Empire imminent, communal forces raised the war cry of secession, encouraged over years by British Divide and Rule policy. Ultimately, to suit their strategic interest, British chose to Divide and Quit. The vivisection of India took place and Pakistan seceded from India. This was not the first vivisection of our country. A thousand years earlier Afghanistan had seceded from India for similar religious reasons. The threat of secession from feudal forces was overcome by the great Sardar. Today, we must at all costs ensure that no third vivisection or partition of India ever takes place.

In 1947, residual India was still a very large country with the second largest population in the world. There were many prophets of doom who felt that such a large behemoth with such multi-religious, multi-lingual and multi-ethnic population will not be able to hold together. It would soon break up under the weight of internal contradictions. On the other hand, Pakistan a much smaller country, united by a strong religious bond was expected to remain intact. Facts turned out to be otherwise with India retaining its unity and Pakistan getting broken up. More than half the population of Pakistan seceded and a new nation State of Bangladesh was born.

Although we have kept our national territory intact during the last six decades, we have had to deal with several secessionist movements. Some of these have been overcome and some continue to pose a serious challenge to us. We faced linguistic secessionism in the South, tribal and political secessionism in North East and religious secessionism in North. During my Army career of forty years and in my post Army career of eleven years as Governor, first of Assam and then of Jammu and Kashmir, I have had to face secessionist challenges. I shall draw upon my personal experience while discussing secessionist movements.

The language agitation against Hindi that started in Tamil Nadu during the first decade after Partition could lead to serious consequences. This agitation was not violent or militant. It was overcome democratically. Democracy has great resilience in containing dissent. The enthusiasm of Hindi chauvinists and Tamil protestors was dowsed through the three language formula. Our federal set up also helped in not allowing matters to get out of hand. The anti-Hindi agitation remained confined to Tamil Nadu. The other non-Hindi speaking States in the South were not affected. Our debacle in the Himalayas of 1962 generated patriotic fervour throughout the country including Tamil Nadu. The Green Revolution that took place soon thereafter, gave us confidence and pride as a nation. Thus, the threat of linguistic secession receded in India. However, in Pakistan linguistic secessionism took a heavy toll.

Tribal secessionist movements erupted in North East, first in Naga Hills followed by Manipur and Mizoram with a spill over effect in the two tribal districts of Assam. The root cause for the movements in these States was that the tribal people had not been fully assimilated in Indian culture and civilization. Insurgency in Nagaland has been contained with cease fire holding for thirteen years and negotiations are taking place to find a political solution. The people of Nagaland have developed a vested interest in peace. The secessionist movement in

Mizoram was overcome through a political solution. The leader of Mizo insurgency, Laldenga was installed as Chief Minister of the State. Today Mizoram is the most peaceful State in North East. The ongoing militancy in Manpur is a matter of concern but it affects only a small fringe area on our border and a small segment of our population. One complexity about Manipur is the fact that one third of the population is of Nagas and Kukis with two third of landspace. One third of land space in the Valley is with Meteis who constitute two third of the State's population. Violence continues to erupt there periodically but the situation is not very serious and we should be able to find a solution in due course. The militancy in Tripura is more in the nature of an ethnic conflict than a secessionist movement. The indigenous tribal population has been reduced to a minority in the wake of influx of Hindu refugees from erstwhile East Pakistan. Compared to other militancy affected States in North East, the level of violence is low. In due course the problem should get resolved politically.

Unlike other tribal secessionist movements in the North East, the ULFA movement in Assam has been essentially political, born out of a feeling of neglect and discrimination. Assamese had reasons to feel neglected. They were woefully short of power and suffered from floods every year. The new temples of India were being constructed at Bhakra Nangal, Damodar, Hirakud and so on. No hydel project had been put up in Assam. They had all the oil wealth of the country till the off shore oil was found. British had built an oil refinery at Digboi in Assam in the beginning of the Twentieth century. After Independence the oil refinery for Assam oil was built at Barauni in Bihar, despite protests in Assam. Tea gardens in Assam were purchased by Marwaris from the British and their corporate offices are in Kolkata. They pay taxes in Bengal. The labour in tea gardens is from Bihar, Orissa and Madhya Pradesh. They send their remittances to their homes. Assam does not get anything from the tea industry. In 1962, when Chinese reached the Foothills near Tezpur, Jawaharlal Nehru in his broadcast stated: "my heart goes out to the people of Assam". This was misinterpreted as a good-bye message as if India was abandoning Assam. All these grievances were simmering for some time. They exploded when it was discovered when in, Mangaldoi constituency of

Assam voters list contained names of 70,000 illegal immigrants from Bangladesh. The Congress party for decades had been encouraging the influx of illegal migrants from East Pakistan/ Bangladesh into Assam as part of vote bank politics. In the Sixties. BK Nehru the then Governor of Assam and his Chief Minister BP Chaliha, an old guard Congressman, had taken up the matter but were overruled by Delhi. In his autobiography, Nice Guys Finish Second, BK Nehru laments saying that for the old generation of Congressmen, national interests were supreme but now the Congress believed in the primacy of party interests. BK Nehru was an eminent member of the dynasty. He cannot be accused of being anti-Congress. On 10 April 1990, Hiteshwar Saikia the Congress Chief Minister had stated on the floor of the State Assembly that there were 3 milliom illegal Bangladeshi migrants in Assam. Two days later he did a complete somersault under pressure and told the Press that there was not a single illegal Bangladeshi migrant in Assam! Insurgency in Assam is far more serious than in other States of the North East. Assam abuts the narrow Siliguri corridor. The letter has great geostrategic importance as it provides the only land link from the Indian mainland to all States of the North East. If the siliguri corridor is lost, the entire North East landmass will be cut off from the rest of India and our borders in the East will have to be redrawn. Economically, Assam is a rich State with its oil and tea wealth, water and mineral resources.

We have also faced religious secessionist movements in our two Northern States, Punjab and Jammu and Kashmir. The centuries of unique history of Hindu-Sikh amity came under serous attack from Sikh extremists. They tried to exploit religious fanaticism and political aspirations to start a movement for a separate State of Khalistan. Their secessionist demand found ready support from Zia-ul-Haq, the Punjabi mulla in khaki, who was only too willing to go all out to help them. He was seeking revenge against India for Pakistan's debacle in 1971. The secessionist movement in Punjab lasted for a decade resulting in the loss of thousands of innocent lives. Both sikh and hindu the total mishandling of Operation Blue Star provided much fuel for the secessionist movement. The assassination of Indira Gandhi made matters worse with large scale anti-Sikh riots in Delhi and a few other places in the country. Ultimately this movement was quelled. The real credit must go to brave people of the State. There were other considerations which also led to this success. The "beti-roti" relationship between the two religious communities and centuries old tradition of amity asserted themselves. Sikhs are the most prosperous and integrated minority in the country and their prosperity is not limited to Punjab only. They have high stakes in States outside Punjab. Democratic process in the State catered for meeting the political aspirations of Sikhs. Punjab Police under the leadership of KPS Gill made a significant contribution in combating violence. All these factors led to ultimate solution of the Punjab crisis.

Secessionist movement in Kashmir, is one of the most complex problems in the world. This issue has been festering since Independence defying solution. Kashmir problem has international, political and religious dimensions. Pakistan's fanatic attachment to grabbing Kashmir by hook or by crook has persisted since 1947. It has fought four wars in Kashmir and has been fighting an ongoing proxy war through exporting terrorism. Letter K in Pakistan stands for Kashmir. Pakistanis fervently believe that it is incomplete without Kashmir. They are paranoid on this score. They want Kashmir to be a part of that country at all cost. The argument that Pakistan was created to provide a homeland for Muslims and an adjacent Muslim majority territory, must not be allowed to remain excluded from it, carries some weight. The West for its own reasons during the Cold War and now during the war on terror finds it convenient to be supportive of Pakistan. Both legally and morally, India has an irrefutable case for Kashmir being an integral part of India. Maharaja's signing of the Instrument of accession trienty met legal requirement. Sheikh Abdulla and his party commanding overwhelming majority in the State, endorsing this accession, provided moral justification. I have been associated with Kashmir from Day One, that is 27 October 1947 when the first lot of Indian troops landed in Srinagar. I was the Secretary of the Indian delegation to UN for delineating Cease Fire Line in 1949. As a soldier I served for several years in war and peace in all the three regions of Kashmir and I was also Governor of Jammu and Kashmir for five years. I am afraid successive Governments have mishandled the Kashmir problem. We have no plan to resolve the issue beyond constantly stating that Kashmir is an integral part of India. Since early eighties, there has been surfeit of petro dollars with fundamentalist Islamic countries. Islamist forces have become strong all over the world and Jehadi terrorism is their instrument of war. Religious fundamentalism is the mainspring for the secessionist movement in Kashmir.

Militancy was at its peak in Assam when I took over as Governor of the State. The Chief Minister had a miraculous escape from a bomb explosion directed at him in Guwahati. In separate incidents, one Minister was killed and another seriously injured. The Chief Secretary and the DGP had deserted. An IG Police and a Brigadier had been killed in two different instances in Guwahati. Two Colonels had been shot inside Kamakhya temple. There were explosions on railway tracks derailing two main passenger trains, the Brahmaputra Mail and North East Express, as a result of which a few hundred passengers were killed. Road and rail communication to Assam were getting disrupted due to explosions damaging road and rail culverts. There had been ethnic violence between Bodos and Adivasis in which 700 people had been killed. Some 2 lakhs Bodos and Adivasis were living in refugee camps. Militants killed in encounters with the Security Forces were hailed as martyrs with large crowds attending their funeral and funeral orations made eulogising them. Guwahati was a dead city and people were afraid to venture out of their houses after dark. Afternoon receptions were not held at Raj Bhavan on Independence and Republic Days because guests returning home in the evenings would be unsafe. I had been given the green signal at Delhi to have President's rule in Assam, if I considered that necessary. I felt that it would be better and more lasting if a solution could be found while a popular government was in power. I found the Chief Minister, Prafulla Kumar Mahanta keen to quell militancy. There was complete synergy of views between us. I discarded the option of President's rule.

I worked on a three prong strategy to combat militancy. Three prongs were unified command, economic development and psychological initiatives. After over forty years of insurgency, for the first time, a unified command was established in the

North East. The Army, Paramilitary and Police now worked as complimentary and not as competing forces. This produced the desired result. The back of militancy was broken. 2500 militants were killed in encounters and over 3000 surrendered with weapons. Over Rs 1 crore in cash was recovered from the militants. Bhutan Army wiped out the terrorist camps in their country. ULFA was down and out.

Various development programmes were undertaken, the most spectacular being installation of one lakh shallow tube wells in Brahmaputra Valley which turned Assam from a rice deficit to a rice surplus State. The Green Revolution had not come to Assam. Agriculture in Assam was still dependent solely on the monsoon and there used to be one crop a year in the State. The crops suffered damage from floods every year. Cultivable land used to remain fallow in the non-monsoon period for want of water for irrigation. Water table in Brahmaputra Valley is high. Shallow tube wells could be put up at low cost. One shallow tube well cost Rs 20,000 only. With the successful completion of this project, Assam started having two to three crops a year. This was a mini green revolution in the State.

Priority was given to psychological initiatives. I decided to tackle the main cause for the alienation of people which lay at the root of the ongoing insurgency. I sent a 42 page printed report to the President on illegal migration from Bangladesh, pointing out that this was not only changing the demography of the State but was also a grave threat to our national security. I recommended various measures to check this menace. This included the repeal of the IMDT Act, which facilitated illegal migration. My report was serialized in every newspaper of Assam and took the people by storm. This was the first time that this issue had been taken up officially by someone in authority. I started being referred to as our man in Raj Bhavan. I decided to have a high emotive content in our psychological initiatives. Little was known about them outside Assam. I had documentaries prepared on their lives and these were shown on Doordarshan national channel. A statue of Lachit Borphukan was installed at the National Defence Academy at Pune and a gold medal in his name was instituted for the best cadet in officer like qualities. Lachit had decisively defeated a Mughal Army of nearly one lakh in the battle of Saraighat in 1671. This was during the reign of Aurangzeb the Mughal military power was at its zenith. Guwahati airport was named after Lokpriya Gopinath Bordoloi. Fifty years after his death, Bordoloi was awarded a posthumous Bharat Ratna. His life size statue was installed in the Lok Sabha. These measures touched the emotional chord of people of Assam. The real measure of our success in Assam was in the mind change that we were able to bring about in the process of winning heart and mind of the people. This was reflected in two episodes. Over a period of time, 81 militants were caught by unarmed villagers in rural areas. Half of them were lynched and the other half handed over to Police. The other very significant episode was the surrender of a large contingent of ULFA which I took on the ULFA Raising Day at Sibsagar Grounds where the ULFA had been raised. This was watched by an appreciative audience of over 10,000. We had isolated the ULFA from the people and had won and mind of the people. In 2003 I left Assam to take over another challenge in Kashmir. When I left Assam I was referred to in the newspapers as a true son of the soil of Assam.

Unfortunately, the gains achieved in combating militancy in Assam by 2003 got squandered away by a misguided policy of appeasement. Congress came to power in the State in the last two years of my tenure in Assam. Tarun Gogoi became the Chief Minister. He openly criticized me for my stand on illegal immigrants from Bangladesh. However, he never raised this issue with me and our relations were otherwise very correct. After I left Assam, Congress came to power also at the Centre. ULFA remnants were surrounded by the Army in jungles in Upper Assam. The Army was asked to lift the cordon and a cease fire was ordered. Talks were started through a People's Consultative Group to get ULFA to agree to a political settlement. The wisdom of having talks and indirect at that time, was debatable as militant organization had been almost totally broken and isolated from the people.

ULFA was only playing for time to rest and regroup. It now got a second lease of life. After more than a year of indirect negotiations nothing came out of them. IMDT Act was struck down by the Supreme Court quoting my report in its judgment. It was brought in again through backdoor by amending the Foreigner's Act. It is rumoured that in 2006, ULFA was given a large amount for not disturbing the national games. ULFA was again on the rampage in Assam. We now seem to be back to square one in Assam but with a difference. ULFA acts of violence do not have the support of people. It is amusing that Tarun Gogoi who had been playing down illegal migration now expressed concern over the activities of HUJI in Lower Assam at the Chief Minister's conference in 2009. HUJI is an Islamist outfit of mostly Bangladeshi immigrants and it has ISI links.

I shall now recount my tenure as Governor in Jammu and Kashmir from June 2003 to June 2008. After the Assembly elections of 2002, the political climate started improving in Kashmir. The level of violence was still high. On average, ten people were getting killed every day. Five weeks before I took over, Vajpayee had made a dramatic statement extending a hand of friendship to Pakistan. This was welcomed by everyone and a little later composite dialogue was started with Pakistan. In November 2003, Pakistan agreed to a cease fire on the LOC. Although violence level inside the State was still very high things started looking up.

During the first couple of years as Governor in Kashmir, I remained handicapped due to complete lack of synergy between me and the Chief Minister, Mufti Mohammad Sayeed. His daughter Mehbooba was the President of his party. They had blatantly communal and anti-national views. They virtually acted as the spokesmen of separatists. The Army has a large presence in Kashmir. It was very responsive to my suggestions. During this period, I worked through the Army. However, two years later it was the turn of the Congress in the alliance to have a Chief Minister. Ghulam Nabi Azad succeeded Mufti. This brought about a sea change in the situation. There was synergy of views between us and we had very cordial relations.

I again worked on the three prong strategy which had been so successful in Assam. It had to be modified to suit conditions in Kashmir. A unified command already existed in Kashmir but there were organizational infirmities which were rectified. The Army's conduct under very difficult conditions was superb, although there were odd unfortunate incidents. Its human rights record has been much better than of Pakistan Army in Baluchistan and NWFP or the US Army in Iraq and Afghanistan. After the 2005 earthquake, the Army launched a massive operation for rescue, relief and rehabilitation of earthquake victims. The common man in the affected areas was all praise for the Army. He wanted all assistance given through the Army and not the civil administration. Yet the Army would continue to be demonized by separatist politicians constantly demanding demilitarization of Kashmir. I took special measures to project the human face of the Army. 27 October was being observed with hartals and black flags in the Valley. It was on this day in 1947 that the first troops of the Indian Army had landed in Srinagar to rescue the people of Kashmir. Pakistan forces had captured Baramulla subjecting its people to rapine and plunder of the worst type. Both Kashmiri Musliums and Kashmiri Hindus had suffered at the hands of invaders. Indian troops on landing at Srinagar were hailed as saviours and liberators. The separatists had turned these facts on their head. They were propagating that an army of occupation had come into Kashmir which committed atrocities against the freedom fighters and the people of Kashmir. I decided to put the record straight. I got the Army to organize a function at Baramulla on that day. We showed a documentary film at the function covering the events of October-November 1947 in Baramulla. An exhibition of newspaper cuttings of that period, both national and international, was also organized. A few surviving citizens of that period who had witnessed the orgy of 1947 were invited to speak about the events of that time. A 99 year old Italian nun at the local convent was brought in a wheeled chair. She also spoke on that occasion on 27 October 2003. A few months later she died. Towards the end of the function, I would recount what I saw in Baramulla on 8 November 1947, when the Indian Army liberated the town. As the years went by, there was increasing public participation in this annual function. The Army modified its tactics of fighting the militants. Surgical strikes instead of the usual cordon and search operations ensured minimum collateral damage. The level of violence gradually reduced from the average of 10 a day in 2002 to 1 a day by 2008. Tourist arrivals in the Valley made a big quantum jump from 28,000 in 2002 to about 6 lakhs by 2008. This was a good indicator of return of normalcy.

Massive doses of economic aid were provided. In 2004 on his first visit to Kashmir as Prime Minister, Dr Manmohan Singh announced an aid package of 24,000 crores. Per capita central aid in Kashmir has been Rs 11,000 as against about Rs 900 in States like Bihar and Orissa. I had one thousand micro-hydel projects installed, based on water mills. This was on the lines of the shallow tube wells in Assam. Each of these generated 5 to 8 kilowat of electricity providing 30 to 40 light points in remote villages on the mountains, where electric bulb had not been seen before. By day the power was used for grinding corn or operating looms. The beneficiaries of this scheme were mostly Gujjars and Bakherwals, who constitute some 20% of the population of the State. They are not much up by religious fundamentalism and they have been generally loyal to India. I recall that on near completion of installing one thousand micro hydel projects, I had been to inaugurate a project in a village on the mountains near Uri. I had to travel some 20 kilometers by road to the site from the helipad. Every village on the route had the Indian national flag fluttering and the villagers had lined up the road with paper national flags in their hands. These people were all Gujjars and Bakherwals.

We undertook wide ranging measures as part of psychological initiatives to win the hearts and minds of the people. Two Army Public Schools, one each at Rajauri and Anantnag and 50 goodwill schools in remote areas were opened by the Army. Students in batches of 40 to 50 were taken to various places in India like Delhi, Ajmer, Agra, Mumbai and so on, to promote national integration. I invited each group on return to Raj Bhavan and over the years, interacted with over 4000, boys and girls who had been taken on Bharat Darshan. Besides all this, my main emphasis was on promoting Kashmiriyat, which is the treasured heritage of the people of Kashmir. It stands for amity and brotherhood across religious divide. I felt Kashmiriyat was the best weapon for countering religious fundamentalism, the root cause for militancy in the State. I went all out to promote Kashmiriyat. On the commencement of Amarnath Yatra I would offer prayers at the Holy Cave and from there go to place a chadar on the grave of Kashmir's patron saint, Sheikh Nurudin at Charar-e-Shareef. We organized three days Sufi music festival at the beginning of the Yatra. For the first time musicians from Pakistan and other countries like Egypt, Syria and Uzbekistan partrijoatd. I started a

Department of Kashmir studies in the Kashmir University. I inaugurated a seminar on Kashmiriyat in the University for which we invited scholars from Pakistan and Central Asian countries. Their participation in the seminar had a healthy impact. In the last fortnight of my stay in Kashmir, we had a big function to promote Kashmiriyat in SAARC countries. The President of India presided over the function. Distinguished delegates from all the eight SAARC countries came for the occasion. Chandrika Kumartunga Bandarnaike came from Sri Lanka, Dr Ghaznafar a senior Cabinet Minister from Afghanistan, Begum Salima Hashmi daughter of the legendary Urdu poet Faiz Ahmed Faiz came from Pakistan and so on. Never before such a high level international function had been held in Kashmir. Despite the separatists call for a boycott of the function, university auditorium with a capacity of 2000 was jam packed. The following day we organized a concert of Sufi pop music by the famous Junoon band from Pakistan. The separatists also called for a boycott of this function and the terrorists even held out threats. Ignoring the boycott call, an audience of several thousands came to listen to the band in the open ground near the Dal Lake. Salman Ali the leader of the band announced that he had come from Pakistan to launch a musical Jehad for peace. The leading English daily of Pakistan, Dawn wrote in an editorial on 28 May 2008, "music knows no boundaries......the people of Kashmir expressed their anger against religious militants and their violence."

Our success in promoting Kashmiriyat rattled the separatist and anti-national politicians with no scruples. 100 acres of waste land at Baltal remains covered in snow for eight months in a year and was traditionally used for tented base camp for pilgrims trekking up to the Amarnath cave. While the ownership of the land was to remain with the State Government, the land was allowed to be used by the Shrine Board for putting up temporary prefabricated shelters. Government order in this regard was issued with the unanimous approval of the State Cabinet. This happened at the same time as our mega Kashmiriyat functions in Srinagar. The separatists used this non-issue of diversion of land at Baltal, to raise a communal tornado saying Hindus were being brought by the Shrine Board to change the demography of the Valley. In this theatre of the absurd, Ministers of the PDP in the Government who had processed and sanctioned the diversion of the land also joined in the agitation. A communal tornado was building up. My five year tenure being over, I left Kashmir. Within days, this tornado was raging in full swing with much violence and loss of property. There was prolonged counter agitation in Jammu at the end of which status quo ante was restored and the Shrine Board permitted to construct temporary shelters.

I have given in some detail how we faired in tackling secessionism in Assam and in Jammu and Kashmir when I was the Governor of those States. This has been done so that we can learn from what happened in those States and profit from it. I would like to stress that we as a Nation have always had a defensive outlook. We suffer from what I call a Panipat syndrome. We must be prepared to take offensive action. There is no reason why we should not take action against terrorist camps in Bangladesh or POK. There is no risk of nuclear escalation as a result of any action in Bangladesh. Top ULFA leaders are known to be operating from Dhaka for decades but we have not done anything about it. After wiping out the LTTE, Sri Lanka picked up Kumaran, the successor of Prabhakaran from Kuala Lampur within a few weeks. The risk of nuclear war has been paralysing us in taking action against Pakistan. However, Pakistan is not deterred by our nuclear power or the risk of nuclear war while pursuing its strategy of thousand cuts to bleed India to death. With a friendly Government in Bangladesh, let us hope the need for any offensive action in Bangladesh may not now arise. As for Pakistan, it is in such a mess of its own creation, that one does not know what course the future may take there. Even if we did not take action against terrorist camps in POK, there was no reason why we should not have paid back Pakistan in its own coin in Northern Area now redesignated Gilgit Baltistan.

The secessionist movements we are facing in these two States should not be viewed in isolation. We need to take note of some of the reports coming from our two big neighbours, ill disposed towards us. A think tank in China has advocated a strategy to break up India into several parts. I am mentioning this to underscore that these secessionist movements have an international dimension. I am not a war monger but I certainly want to stress the need for a high degree of military preparedness to deal with both external and internal challenges to our national security. We must maintain our borders inviolate. Hitherto, we have been negligent in our military preparedness. We must wake up and make up for lost time in terms of infrastructure and military strength. Apart from secessionist movements and external threats, we also have to deal with extreme left wing terrorists. The policy of appeasement or playing party politics with national security will not do. We should not allow ourselves to be perceived as a soft State with no strategic doctrine which is incapable of taking hard decisions.

10

TWO FRONT STRATEGY

Pakistani media and strategic community was in fits over General Deepak Kapoor's statement on two front strategy. His earlier statement about the possibility of a conventional war between nuclear weapon powers also drew much flak. Pakistani media treated the two front strategy as virtual declaration of war against Pakistan. Interestingly, Ayaz Amir a liberal Pakistani journalist of The News, found nothing wrong in it.

In 1950, the Chinese Army moved into Tibet. Despite the then cordial relations between India and China, Sardar Patel in his letter of 17 November 1950 to Jawaharlal Nehru warned him of the danger that then lurked in the North. Four weeks later, the great Sardar died. Nehru chose to ignore his warning. He told General Cariappa, the then Army Chief to focus on Pakistan and he would deal with China. The Army worked on a one front strategy which cost us a humiliating defeat in 1962.

The Indo-Soviet treaty of friendship kept China at bay. Thus, desperate pleadings of the beleaguered Pakistan Army in East Pakistan for Chinese intervention, remained unheeded. Given the above history and Pakistan's ongoing proxy war as also increasing Chinese belligerence, it will be an act of madness for India, not have a two front strategy. In fact, after 26/11, we also need to focus on our coast line, which is now a third front.

General Kapoor's statement on two front strategy is perfectly legitimate and fully justified. It was being deliberately misrepresented in Pakistan to promote a war psychosis. Pakistan Government's official spokesman has asked the world to take due note of India's alleged hegemonic and hostile intentions. Foreign Minister Mohammad Qureshi has called Kapoor's statement absurd and very irresponsible. General Tariq Majid, Chairman Joint Chiefs of Staff called it outlandish saying, "Leave alone China, General Deepak Kapoor knows very well that Indian Armed Forces cannot and Pakistan Armed Forces can pull off militarily". General Kyani has talked of Pakistan Army suitably dealing with Indian military adventurism. A defence analyst in Pakistan sees in General Kapoor's statement, a shift in civil-military relations in India, with the weight moving in favour of military. Another has enquired if Delhi is preventing a fourth battle of Panipat or instigating it. Whereas reactions in Pakistan were hysterical, it is significant that there has been no reaction or comments from China on this issue. Every country needs to have a strategy for defending its frontier in the worst case scenario. If it had been stated that India was planning to force a two front strategy on Pakistan, such virulent reaction from Pakistan would be understandable. The war hysteria in Pakistan is being deliberately generated with a purpose. This could be to find an excuse for not moving troops from Pakistan's eastern front to pursue the war on terror with greater vigour, or to get the USA to resolve the Kashmir issue on Pakistan's terms or to get more aid from its super power benefactor for improving its military strength against India. The third possibility has been working well. Pakistan's long standing demand for drones has at last been conceded. And now Pakistan Prime Minister gleefully asserts that India has been forced to come to the conference table.

In thousands years of its history, India has never invaded any country nor coveted any foreign territory. Ashoka the Great, the unique Prince of Peace, propagated world peace, the like of which was never attempted by any other ruler in the history of mankind. He did this from a position of military strength. After Independence, India tried to do so from a position of military weakness. This led to the debacle of 1962. The impregnability of the Himalayas, the invincibility of our Army and the infallibility of our foreign policy got shattered. Today, as never before, we need to promote peace from a position of military strength.

11

RESOLVING THE KASHMIR ISSUE

Kashmir has been a festering problem for the last 63 years. We have no road map for resolving this issue. We merely assert that Kashmir is an integral part of India and a solution will emerge through dialogue. We suffer from lack of strategic vision, remaining unprepared to face crises and not learning from the past.

We have blundered from one folly to another on Kashmir and have been repeatedly scoring self-goals. There was a common Instrument of Accession drafted for all Princely States to accede to either India or Pakistan. Jinnah had been the attorney of the Khan of Kalat. On 4 August 1947 a written agreement was signed by Mountbatten, Jinnah and the Khan that on 14 August 1947, Baluchistan will become independent. Yet in January 1948 the Khan on a visit to Karachi was forced to sign he instrument of Accession with no special provisions as in the case of Kashmir. Immediately thereafter, insurgency erupted in Baluchistan which continues to this day. In October 1947, with the enemy closing on Srinagar, a desperate Maharaja signed the instrument of accession. Yet strangely, through exchange of letters we agreed to special provisions for Kashmir which put Kashmir on a different footing from all erstwhile Princely States that acceded to India or Pakistan. That was our initial folly. This was followed by taking up the Kashmir issue in the United Nations. During the 1947-48 war, the Army was not allowed to exploit its success on three occasions in Novembers 1947, in June 1948 and in December 1948. Had the Army not been prevented, Muzaffrabad and POK would have been in our hands today. After the 1965 war we returned the strategic Hajipur pass to Pakistan on a platter at Tashkent and after the 1971 war, we were outwitted at Shimla. We surrendered our gains without securing a settlement of the Kashmir problem. When militancy erupted in Kashmir in 1989 we failed to highlight that it was a totally communal movement. The international community may not have been in a mood to listen to us then, but surely after 9/11 a vigorous drive on this would have found the world receptive. Although our Parliament passed a unanimous resolution wanting the state territory in illegal possession of Pakistan to be liberated, we did nothing about it. We have been ignoring Gilgit Balistan where the people rebelled against Pakistan. Apart from Pakistan treating this region as a colony and changing its demography, increasing penetration of China with road and railway construction activities and also building Army barracks for its Soilders have added another dimension of the problem. We allow kashmiri separatists to maintain close contact with the Pakistan mission in Delhi and meet visiting Pakistani dignitaries but our mission in Islamabad and our visiting dignitaries to Pakistan, do not contact any leaders from Gilgit Balistan. We agreed to have Srinagar-Muzaffrabad opened but could not get road Kargil-Skardu opened. Our follies in Kashmir have been endless. In 2009 the UPA was so mesmerized by its agenda of installing youth in power, ignoring local sentiments. It got Omar Abdulla made the Chief Minister. Through acts of omission and commission, he has allowed the situation in the Valley to spin out of control. In retrospect, it would have been much better if the experienced and locally more acceptable senior Abdulla, had been allowed to become the Chief Minister.

Apart from relentless hostility towards India, Pakistan has a pathological obsession about Kashmir. It tried wars in 1947, 1965, 1971 and 1999 but could not succeed. It has been trying terrorism for twenty years but even that has not succeeded. The new strategy since 2008 has been to generate a mass movement to secure secession. Amarnath controversy based on total falsehood and fraud generated a communal tornado. The same tactics of falsehood and fraud was tried again in 2009 in regard to the so called rape and murder of two young women at Shopian. Amarnath and Shopian were rehearsals for generating mass movements by exploiting an emotive issue, to arouse frenzy for Azadi. It was the religious card in 2008, Kashmiri honour in 2009 and youngster getting killed as a result of Police firing in 2010. Whereas, the first two were based on falsehood the latter is based on manufactured facts. The stone pelting operations were started to time with Indo-Pak Foreign Minister' talks. It is continuing and the pot is likely to be kept boiling till a full blown intifada erupts in November, during Obama's visit. Obama desperately seeking exit from Afghanistan with honour for which Pakistan support is vital, may be only too willing to help Pakistan on Kashmir. The media promotes sympathy for the "innocent" young boys pelting stones. It is said that the young generation in the Valley has grown up in violence and is angry because of lack of employment opportunities. The young generation in poonch, Rajauri and Doda, leave alone Jammu, Kargil and Leh, has also grown up in a similar manner, but has not resorted to stone throwing. Day in and day out, we see pictures of wailing women and funeral processions of victims of police firing in the media. It is hardly ever mentioned that over 1400 of our Security Force personnel have been injured, many grievously, due to stone pelting. The stone pelting is part of an international Jihad agenda. The chant of the crowds in the Valley is, "Ham Kya Chahte, Azadi: Azadi ka kya matlab, La Ilahi Illila."

Jammu and Kashmir has a very diverse demography. Separatist sentiments and separatist violence are confined to a large segment of Kashmiri Muslims but not to all. Non-Kashmiri Muslims like Gujars, Bakherwals and Kargil Shias plus non-Muslims constitute 60% of the State's population. They do not nature anti-national sentiments. Yet all our thinking is Kashmir centric and not Jammu and Kashmir centric. opinion polls conducted by foreign agencies have been revealing. In 2002 Mori poll of UK under the patronage of Lord Avebury, a known protagonist of Pakistan, found that 61% Kashmiris Wanted to remain in India, 33% were undecided and 6% wanted to join Pakistan. A poll conducted in may 2010 by King's College London University at the instance of the son of colonel Gadaffi, found that only 2% of Kashmiris opted for Pakistan. The minority with generous assistance from across the border us holding the majority in Kashmir to ransom.

Religious fundamentalism is the root cause for militancy in Kashmir. It has become deep rooted and Kashmir's Sufi heritage has got largely marginalized. Sufi sentiments are still alive in Kashmir but those believing in Sufism are not allowed to assert themselves. In 1990 they had to remain silent spectators to the ethnic cleansing of nearly 5 lakh Kashmiri Pandits. Now the Sikhs in the Valley have been asked to convert to Islam or quit the Valley.

Economic development in the face of religious fanaticism has little impact. The highest per capita outlay of the Central Government is in Kashmir. It is ten times more than many other States. People living below poverty line in Kashmir, has come down from 25% to 3.7% as against the national average of 26%. As for employment, 11% of Kashmir's population is in government jobs as against the national average of 2%. If industries have not flourished in the State, it is because under Article 370, outsiders cannot acquire land there.

Pakistan and her friends, notably China and the separatists in Kashmir, maintain that Kashmir is a disputed territory. There is no basis for this assertion. Kashmir acceded to India in a perfectly legal manner in accordance with the Indian Independence Act of 1947 passed by the British Parliament. The united Nations duly recognized this in its 13 August 1948 resolution providing for complete withdrawal of Pakistan forces from Kashmir while the Indian Army was to remain there, pending plebiscite. Had it been otherwise, a UN force may have been organized for Kashmir till plebiscite was held. Again in 1949, while delineating the cease fire line, 200 square miles of No Man's Land in Tilel Valley was handed over to India and not shared between India and Pakistan. And again, if Kashmir is a disputed territory, how come Pakistan has gifted 2,000 square miles of State territory in the North to China? Plebiscite could not be held because of Pakistan's intransigence in not adhering to its commitment to withdraw her forces from Kashmir. Today, it has become irrelevant because unlike India, Pakistan has changed the demography of the territory in its illegal occupation by setting Punjabis and Pothobaris there. However, the people have had opportunities to express their preference by supporting the Indian Army during the 1965 war. The Pakistan Commander-in-Chief during that war, General Musa in his book, My Vision, has lamented that they could not win that war in Kashmir because the people did not support them. Elections in Kashmir have been an endorsement by the people of Kashmir's accession to India, despite the boycott call by separatists. The lid on the allegation of rigged election was blown off in 2002 and 2008, which were hailed by international media as free and fair. In both these elections, ruling party in the State lost and so did the ruling party at the Centre in 2002. The massive voter turn out in Assembly elections of 2008 and Parliamentary elections of 2009, well above the national average, particularly after the summer madness in the wake of Amaranth controversy and despite the boycott calls, was an endorsement of India's stand in Kashmir. Of course, separatists argue that elections cannot be a substitute for plebiscite or self determination. Even if one was to accept this tenuous argument, the voter turn out in these elections shows how little support separatists have among the people. In Assam when the separatists gave a boycott call during 1983 election, the voter turnout was a mere 3%.

We must have a proper road map for resolving the Kashmir issue and pursue that with determination. Half hearted measures or policy of drift and appeasement will not get us anywhere.

Our immediate priority is to restore writ of State in the Valley, at all Costs. Unfortunately, Omar Abdulla has become a hate figure in Kashmir. In his own interest, he should have resigned. That would have helped him to stage a political come back later. The longer he stays in power, the more harmful it may be for him and for India. His opponents project him as a puppet of Delhi, like some earlier Chief Ministers of the benighted State. This fans the agitation further. If a replacement for him cannot be found through a transparent democratic process, let there be Governor's rule in the State. (There is no provision for president's rule in Jammu and Kashmir as in order State). The district administration is in shambles. Effective Deputy Commissioners not prone to local influence should be positioned forthwith. Twelve Police stations have been burnt down by the miscreants and the State Police is demoralised. Some Policemen have even shown sympathy for the separatists. This problem has to be addressed ruthlessly. Police discipline and morale must be restored. The Police must be equipped with modern protective gear against stone pelting. It should also have modern non-lethal weapons for crowd dispersal, like water cannon, rubber bullets, stun grenades and so on. Delay of years in obtaining these has been unpardonable. Large scale preventive detention of trouble makes has become a necessity. Firing should be opened only as a last resort and it should be with a view to disable and not to kill. The game plan of the separatists is to provoke the Police to open fire and get youngsters killed to arouse popular resentment. Political and religious leaders should reach out to the people to restore sanity and avoidable loss of young lives. There are now signs of people getting tired of living under prolonged curfew and wanting normalcy to be restored, so that shops can open and normal life resumed. Advantage should be taken of this. Hopefully, Police and Paramilitary in Kashmir can regain control over the situation. It is desirable that the Army be kept out of these operations. However if the Police and the Paramilitary fail to restore the situation, there will be no alternative but to send for the Army. A worse situation with large scale terrorist violence and mass upheaval combined with ethnic cleansing of Kashmiri Pandits and vandalising of Hindu temples, was successfully tackled by the Army in 1990. The slogan renting the Valley then was Kashmir Banega Pakistan. This was not allowed to happen.

Without curbing freedom of the Press, the support of the media should be enlisted to counter false anti-India propaganda and project our national stand on Kashmir in a positive and convincing manner, both internationally and with in Kashmir. Unfortunately, this has been ignored and we have faired badly in the media war. The media in Kashmir has been demonizing the Army when Indian Army's record in Kashmir has been far superior to that of Pakistani Army in Baluchistan and Wazirstan; leave alone the mass genocide in erstwhile East Pakistan. Difference between the Indian and Pakistani approach needs to be highlighted. Unlike Pakistan in Baluchistan and Waziristan, and the US in Iraq and Afghanistan, India has never used air strike or artillery, against militants in Kashmir. An Indian Major was accused of rape in Handwara. He was court martialed and dismissed, even the rape could not be proved, because it was proved that he had been to the woman in her house at night and this conduct was unbecoming of an officer. At the same time, a Pakistan Army Major was accused of raping a lady doctor in a Quetta hospital. No action was taken against the Major. Widespread disturbances in Baluchistan were quelled ruthlessly by the Pakistan Army. The Lady Doctor migrated to Canada. Musharraf made a light of the whole thing saying "Get raped, Get Money and Get Visa to Canada". Another comparison between Indian and Pakistani approach is also telling. The inveterate separatist leader Syed Ali Shah Geelani was reported terminally ill with cancer of lever. He wanted to go to US for treatment but the US Government denied him visa because of his terrorist links. He was treated in Mumbai by Indian doctors who performed a miraculous surgery and saved his life. Mohammed Akbar Bugti the veteran separatist leader of Baluchistan was in a hideout. On receiving intelligence of this, Musharraf ordered an air strike which killed Bugti.

Some years ago, one Super Power succumbed to Jehadi terrorism in Afghanistan and another with its exit strategy is in the process of following suit. It is in the interest of the international community not to allow Jihad to succeed in Kashmir. This will only pave the way for a Nizam-e-Mustafa to be eventually established in the world. Our external publicity needs to constantly highlight this. Within Kashmir, Sufi sentiments need to be revived. The most revered Sufi shrine of Kashmir at Charar-e-Shareef was burnt down by Mast Gul, a terrorist from Pakistan. Repeated attacks on revered Sufi shrines have been taking place in Pakistan. The famous Seventeenth Century Sufi Shrine of Ram Baba at the foot of Khyber Pass was dynamited out of existence recently. In May this year, a Sufi cultural centre at Perus in Lahore was bombed during the annual Sufi music festival. On 2 July 2010, the most reverted and the largest Sufi Shrine in Pakistan, Datta Saheb in Lahore, was attacked while people were offering their prayers;

resulting in 42 deaths and 175 injured. On 25 october 2010, Saint Farid's Shrine at Pakpathan, South of Lahore ad Fired killing 6 women and 26 worshippess were including women and children. Offering prayers at Ziarats (graves of Sufi Saints) is still very popular in Kashmir. Wahabi Mullas maintain that grave worshippers are apostates. Sufi sentiments need to be mobilized in fight against religious foundamentalism.

No doubt, a political solution is imperative for ultimately resolving the Kashmir problem. Political parleys with leaders can take place only after the raging fire in Valley is brought under control. For the Round Table Conference, Mirwaiz refused to sit with other leaders whom he called "Tom Dick and Harry" and now Mehbooba Mufti has repeatedly spurned the Prime Minister's invitation for talks. If Sheikh Abdulla could be kept in detention and deported outside the state for nearly twenty years, why can't the sane treatment be meted out to all the present Venom spewing separatists? Once the present situation is brought under reasonable control, talks may be held with all stake holders in the State to fined a solution which will meet aspirations of all the people of the State and not only of seperatists in the Valley.

After the round table talks boycotted by the separatists, we took the bizarre decision of appeasing the PDP which advocates healing touch for the terrorists. Special bounty was provided for families of terrorists killed in encounter with security forces. Such a bizarre arrangement is not there for other terrorists in the country or for that matter anywhere in the world. This constitutes a virtual fillip to terrorism. There is now talk of appeasing the National Conference with accepting its demand of autonomy. Jammu and Kashmir has more autonomy than any other State in India. This new autonomy demand calls for removel of the jurisdiction of the Supreme Court, Election Commission and Comptroller and Auditor General, from the State. The Governor to be a citizen of the State to be elected to his office and there be no central services like the IAS and IPS in the State. This autonomy demand is designed dangerously to erode the sovereignty of India in Kashmir. Appeasement whets appetite only it may be the National Conference Version of the autonomy today, PDP version of self rule (dual currency and joint legislature) tomorrow and azadi or merger with Pakistan, the day after. Prime Minister Narsimha Rao had rightly said that sky was the limit for Kashmir, provided the solution was within the framework of Indian Constitution. Talking of autonomy, there is a crying need for regional autonomy within the State and empowerment of people. Jammu and Kashmir is the only State in country, where Panchayati Raj has not been established and the Right to information Act is not functional.

Kashmir is an internal problem of India and we should not brook interference from any country is Kashmir. Pakistan is our neighbour. We wish Pakistan well and would like to have good relations with her but we should not allow Pakistan any role in Kashmir. Pakistan's illegal occupation of large tract of the State territory has almost gained world acceptability; in the absence of any serious objections raised by India. As for the lone Super Power, whose position of eminence in the world is fast eroding, it should also not have any say in Kashmir. If countries like North Korea and Iran can defy the US, there is no reason why over a billion strong India with all her strength and all her resources, should allow herself to be pressurised by US. What we need is the will and determination to take hard decisions and resolve the Kashmir problem on our own.

12

FAULTLINES IN KASHMIR

The Valley was burning for three months. Over one hundred stone pelting youth got killed. Thanks to governance deficit, both in Srinagar and Delhi, the situation appeared out of control.

Zia-ul-Haq Islamised Pakistan. This spread to Kashmir. In 1990 there was ethnic leansing of over 3 lakh Kashmiri Pandits. Several dozen Hindu temples were destroyed. The plight of Kashmiri Pandits was glossed over. There was a virtual blackout of information about the vandalisation of dozens of temples. In 2007, to appease the PDP, Government took the bizarre decision of providing bounty for families of terrorists killed in encounter with security Forces. This does not happen elsewhere in the country or anywhere else in the world. To appease the NC, Government is considering its demand for autonomy which will undermine the sovereignty of India in Kashmir. The Supreme Court, the Election Commission and Comptroller and Auditor General would not have any jurisdiction in Kashmir. There would be an elected governor from the state with no central services like IAS and IPS in Kashmir. "misguided" young boys in terrorist camps in POK should be allowed to return. PDP under the garb of self rule wants dual currency and a joint State legislature with POK in Kashmir. All this will undermine India's sovereignty in Kashmir.

Pakistan launched repeated conventional wars to grab Kashmir but failed every time. It has also failed in doing so through terrorism. Mass upsurges have been organized. Sine 2008 religious frenzy was aroused in 2008 on the basis of manufactured lies. The 100 acre barren land at Baltal, traditionally used as base camp for Amarnath pilgrims, was diverted to the Shrine Board for 2.2 crores. Ownership of the land remained with the state. The Board could put up only prefabricated shelters for pilgrims. This land is unapproachable and uninhabitable for eight months in a year due to snow. Yet a canard was spread that Hindus were being brought to settle in Baltal and change the demography of the Valley, like Isreal had done in Palestine. The Valley media propagated this. A mass movements of gigantic dimension erupted. To appease the agitators, Government cancelled the land diversion order and ordered virtual disbandment of Shrine Board. After three months of counter agitation in Jammu, Status qua ante was restored. In 2009, two women drowned in a river at Shopian. A mass movement was started on the basis of diabolical concoction of facts about the women being raped and killed by Security Forces. Fraudulent medical reports were prepared and false witnesses produced. The Valley was held to ransom for two months. Ultimately, truth was unraveled by the CBI. Having tested waters in 2008 and 2009, the emotive issue of Azadi was exploited for a mass movement in 2010. "The peaceful" agitation took form of stone pelting. Sympathy was aroused through portraying "young innocent" boys being brutally killed by the Police. Over 2000 Security Force personnel more injured due to stone pelting. This is hardly known, nor the fact that some 1000 Baluchis have been killed by Pakistan Army two years back. Reports in the media of half truths and funeral pictures with grieving family members were inflaming passions. Stone pelting is confined to the Valley. Religious card was used to extend agitation outside the Valley. Protests were organized against Qoran burning, which had not happened. Nowhere else in the Muslim world, violence took place on this score. Stone pelting is claimed to be a spontaneous outburst of angry youth in the Valley. Muslim youth in Poonch, Rajauri, Doda and Kargil living under similar conditions did not take on it.

Kashmir problem has been communalised in the State and by the OIC internationally. Hitherto our Muslims outside Kashmir had kept themselves aloof from the Kashmir issue.

Jamiat-Ulema-Hind held a convention of 10,000 Muslims of all sects at Deoband on 4 October 2010, to express solidarity with Kashmiri Muslims. This can have most dangerous consequences in Muslim majority districts in Bengal, Bihar, Assam and Kerala.

A vigilant Government should have nipped stone pelting in the bud. The Police and paramilitary were ill equipped and ill trained for crowd control. The Government failed to act firmly. The British had restored calm within few weeks of our freedom movements in 1920, 1930 and 1942. During the Black Emergency, Indira Gandhi put one lakh people under preventive detention. Violence did not erupt. Secessionist leaders in Kashmir are free to propagate sedition. Chinese have maintained order in Tibet and Xingiang and so has Pakistan in Baluchistan. Mao stated that revolution is not a dinner party. That applies equally to counter terrorism operations. Delhi sent a Parliamentary delegation to Kashmir only after three months. Some members called on secessionist leaders who had refused to meet the delegation. One of them, a former Cabinet Minister, who had campaigned in election with a double of Osama bin Laden on his side, declared that the ongoing movement in Kashmir has no Pakistani connection.

The Army is being constantly demonized for human rights violations, when its record is far superior to that of the US Army in Iraq and Afghanistan or Pakistan Army in Baluchistan and Waziristan. Unlike them, we have never used air strikes or artillery against militants in Kashmir. We have been taking promptaition against human rights violators. Over the years, 1514 cases against the Army were reported of which, 1470 were found false. Action was taken against 70 individuals, dismissing them from service and awarding imprisonment for 2 to 14 years. India has also been humane in dealing with secessionist leaders. Geelani the veteran secessionist leader, suffering from advanced stage of lever cancer, was refused visa by the US for medical treatment because of his terrorist connection. He went to Mumbai, where Dr Sameer Koul, a Kashmiri Pandit, operated on him, treating him with competence and compassion. On return to Srinagar, he stated that India is in illegal occupation of Kashmir and the international community should impose economic sanction against her. Musharraf ordered air strike in Baluchistan on the hideout of the veteran leader Akbar Bugti. He was killed. To appease the separatists, periodic troop withdrawals have taken place in Kashmir. Now, there is talk of amending or scrapping AFSPA. Confucius wrote, "To know what is right and not do it, is wrost cowardice". Winston Churehill was more biting. He stated, "An appeaser is one who feeds the crocodile, hoping that it will eat him last".

Crying need in Kashmir is to establish writ of State in the Valley forthwith and prevent further communalisation. Without curbing freedom of the press, we should ensure that the media does not act as the mouthpiece of secessionists. The law on sedition must be enforced. Kashmiri Muslims constitute a minority in the State with other Muslims and non-Muslims, being in a majority. Even among Kashmiri Muslims, not all are secessionists. We should politically isolate secessionists from the rest of the people. A political solution acceptable to all, should be evolved through dialogue but this must be strictly within the framework of the Indian Constitution.

PART-III
TERRORISM

13

THE MENACE OF TERRORISM

The biggest menace facing mankind today is terrorism. Millions of innocent lives have been lost due to terrorism in the last half a century. However, terrorism par se is not a new phenomenon in history. Acts of terrorism have been taking place through the ages. The massacres by Chengiz Khan, Timur or Nadir Shah were acts of State terrorism. So were in recent times, the Cultural Revolution in China and the genocide by the Poll Pot regime in Cambodia. In the past, terrorism was practiced by strong against the weak. Of late, world has been witnessing terrorism of weak against the strong. Nine eleven is a classic example. Terrorist groups have been causing large scale casualties of innocent citizens to achieve their nefarious designs. They have unleashed a virtual war against the State and society.

The UN Security Council has defined terrorism as an act intended to cause death of civilians or non-combatants with a view to intimidating the Government or the society in pursuit of political, ideological or religious goals. The latter is often referred to as Jehadi terrorism. Brigadier SK Malik of the Pakistan Army, a favourite of General Zia-ul-Haq known as the Mulla in Khaki, has written a book on the Quranic concept of warfare. He maintains that the human race is divided into two categories of believers and non-believers. The believers must be constantly at war with non-believers till they are killed or they are converted. Striking terror amongst the non-believers must be the constant aim. It is not a means to an end but an end in itself. Through striking terror, the non-believer should lose faith in himself, his religion, his polity and in his State. Ali Qaeda has a similar philosophy. It aims to establish a Caliphate, where Nizam-e-Mustafa will prevail. The world is divided into Dar-ul-Islam and Dar-ul-Harb. In the former, Islam prevails and in the latter, other religions are dominant. Dar-ul-Harb has to be converted into Dar-ul-Islam.

There are three types of terrorism. These are secessionist terrorism, revolutionary, terrorism and religious or Jehadi terrorism. India has been a victim of all these types of terrorism. We have suffered terrorist depredations for much longer than any other country in the world. We have faced secessionist terrorism in North East, revolutionary terrorism of Naxals and both variations of Jehadi terrorism, one in which people's support is available and the other in which it is not. Jehadi terrorism in Kashmir has the support of a sizeable section of the local people. We have also been facing the other version of Jehadi terrorism with virtually no popular support. The repeated terrorist attacks in many of our mainland cities fall in this category. Among these, the 26/11 Mumbai attack was in a class of its own. It was a terror war unleashed by Pakistan against India.

The terrorist is normally an invisible enemy. His strongest weapon is surprise, compounded by his commitment to sacrifice his life. The Jehadi terrorist is thoroughly indoctrinated. He is ever willing to undertake suicide missions. He is convinced that if he sacrifices his life for the holy cause, gates of Heaven and eternal bliss will open for him. When the terrorist gets deluded to believe that he can successfully fight a conventional battle against regular forces, he is destined to fail. The LTTE in Sri Lanka was the most well organized terrorist organization of the world. It had pioneered the concept of suicide attacks. It had naval and air wings and it made good use of them. A worldwide network was available to it, ensuring free flow of funds and weapons. It had a very powerful leader who commanded unquestioned loyalty from its cadres. It over estimated its strength and decided to fight a conventional last ditch battle with Sri Lanka's regular forces. In the process, it got wiped out.

We need to put our record of dealing with terrorism under

the scanner to draw appropriate lessons. While doing so, I shall take the liberty of drawing on my experience as Governor in Assam for six years and thereafter in Jammu and Kashmir for five years. Let me first emphasise that no war has been won by fighting only defensive action. Wars are won through offensive action. Dealing with terrorism through defensive measures alone, cannot eliminate this menace. Matters get further compounded if there are serious flaws in the defensive measures that are undertaken. It is impossible to defend every possible terrorist target. Wide dispersion of resources in trying to defend too many likely terrorist targets can only weaken our ability to deal with the terrorist menace. The Napoleonic maxim that he who tries to be strong everywhere ends up being strong nowhere, is equally true in the war against terror. In the ultimate analysis, success is obtained by destroying the terrorist's capability to attack.

Cross border terrorism started in Kashmir in 1989 and cross border illegal migration in Assam started much earlier. The latter led to insurgency erupting in that State in 1979. Our reaction to the former has been purely defensive and to the latter almost collusive. This has impacted adversely on our security. Training camps of the terrorists and their launching pads in Pakistan Occupied Kashmir are only a few thousand yards away. Yet we failed to carry out surgical strikes across the Line of Control in territory which we claim to be legally ours. We did not even once exercise the right of hot pursuit across the border. We developed cold feet because we did not want another war with Pakistan on our hands. Initially, there was a fear that Pakistan had nuclear bombs in the basement. In 1999 Pakistan became a nuclear weapon State and now we could seek to justify our inaction on the plea of avoiding a nuclear war. On the other hand, Pakistan had no fears of any Indian retaliation and merrily went about pursuing its strategy of thousand cuts. Pakistan had correctly adjudged India as a soft State. Israel has been taking immediate and massive retaliatory action whenever it has been attacked from across its border. The USA sent its forces across oceans and continents in retaliation for 9/11.

Our total casualties in the three and a half wars we fought with Pakistan have been less than 10,000. We have lost three times that number fighting terrorism in Kashmir. Walter Lipman's definition of national security needs to be iterated. "A nation has security when it does not have to sacrifice its legitimate interests to avoid war and is able, if challenged, to maintain them by war". We have been sacrificing our national interests at the altar of an exclusively defensive policy. Secessionist terrorism in Kashmir is essentially a product of religious fundamentalism. Apart from inflicting heavy attrition on militants, we were making progress in curbing religious fundamentalism through promoting Kashmiriyat, which stands for amity across religious divide. Religious fanatics and anti-national forces fearing losing their base, raised a communal tornado over a non-issue in relation to Amarnath Yatra. Sanity overcome the pryudee. Both regions agreed to restore status quoante. At the next Assembly and Parliamentary elections, despite and boycott calls, voters endorsed the settlement. However, Valley Press and the "secular" national media supported communalists. Media in Kashmir is in the hand of Militancy.

Our record of dealing with illegal migration in Assam has been bizarre. For the sake of vote bank politics, the Congress party has been encouraging illegal migration from East Pakistan/Bangladesh into Assam. In late Sixties, Governor BK Nehru and his Chief Minister BP Chaliha raised this issue again but Indra Gandhi had brushed them aride. In his autobiography, Nehru laments, "The East Bengal Muslim was the main vote bank of the Congress party in Assam. Chaliha dating as he did from the days of the freedom struggle was governed by the values of that time. But the High Command thought otherwise, party interests were paramount". In 1993, Lt Gen Jameel Mahmood, the Eastern Army Commander had cautioned the Chief Minister of Assam that if action was not taken to curb the demographic influx from across the border, boundary of India would have to be redrawn in the East. He also represented to Army Headquarters that if the influx was not stopped, the day was not far off when a Kashmir type of situation will develop in Dhubri and adjacent districts of Lower Assam, abutting the narrow Siliguri corridor. All these warnings went unheeded. To facilitate illegal migration from Bangladesh, the Congress passed a special legislation for Assam only, shifting the burden of proof to establish citizenship from the individual to the State along with other such helpful measures for the illegal migrants. This legislation was called IMDT (Illegal Migration Determination by Tribunal) Act. This gave a further impetus to the unabated influx from Bangladesh into Assam. On 10 April 1992, Chief Minister Hiteshwar Saikia declared in the State Assembly that there were 3 million Bangladeshi illegal migrants in Assam. He came under pressure and there was a risk of his Government falling. Two days later he stated to the Press that there was not a single illegal Bangladeshi migrant in Assam. I took over as Governor of Assam in 1997, when secessionist feelings and terrorist violence were at their peak in the State. The root cause for this was the unabated influx of illegal migrants and the Congress encouraging the same for its vote bank. I submitted a 42 paged printed report to the President highlighting that this influx was not only a grave threat to the demography of the State but also a grave threat to our national security. Through co-ordinated military operations we broke the back of ULFA militancy. Their camps in Bhutan were wiped out by the Bhutanese Army. The cumulative effect of all these measures was that secessionist terrorism in Assam was virtually eliminated. There was now a total reversal of public attitude towards the ULFA. 81 militants were caught by villagers over a period of time. Half of them were lynched and the remainder handed over to the Police. Surrender of ULFA and other militants to Security Forces were now being witnessed appreciatively by the local people. That was the real measure of the success we had achieved in dealing with ULFA militancy that had ravaged the State for two decades. To make our success complete, I had been recommending suitable action against the two key ULFA leaders, its President Arbind Rajkhowa and its Commander-in-Chief Paresh Barua, holed up in Dacca. They remained there for nearly twenty years and they had also been travelling to various foreign countries. Yet our intelligence agencies were not able to pick them up. In sharp contrast to our inability to do so, Sri Lankan intelligence agencies, in a matter of weeks, picked up from Kuala Lampur, the newly appointed LTTE Chief Kumaram Pathnanatham who had succeeded Prabhakaran. We never attempted a surgical strike against terrorist camps in Bangladesh, even though there was no threat of any nuclear retaliation or even a conventional war on that account, as in the case of Kashmir.

I completed my six years as Governor of Assam and left for Jammu and Kashmir in 2003. I had the satisfaction of seeing the insurgency in Assam virtually over. During the latter part of my tenure in Assam I had to work with a Congress Chief Minister. He was highly critical of me in public for my views on illegal migration from Bangladesh. To appease his vote bank, he maintained that no infiltration was taking place from across the border. With the Congress now in power at both Delhi and in Guwahati, there was a U turn in Government policy towards the ULFA. Militants of that outfit were on the run and were surrounded by the Army in the jungles of Upper Assam. The Army was ordered to lift their encirclement and cease fire was declared. Fruitless dialogue with the ULFA leaders through intermediaries without much credential, continued for over a year. This allowed the ULFA all the time to regroup and make up their losses. During 2005 Assembly elections, ULFA's help was sought for a price and during National Games of 2006 it is said that the ULFA was compensated for not disturbing the mega sport event. Terrorist violence has now returned to Assam but the redeeming feature is that the ULFA no longer enjoys popular support. At the conference of Chief Ministers in 2009, to say the least, it was amusing to find the same Congress Chief Minister of Assam expressing concern about terrorist violence in Assam by HUJI, a militant communal outfit of Bangladeshis with ISI links.

The Mumbai terror attack of 26/11 was different from previous acts of terrorism in our country sponsored by Pakistan. It was a meticulously planned invasion launched and controlled by our hostile neighbour. The footprints of the State agencies of Pakistan have been revealed. One of the Pakistani terrorists captured alive has provided a wealth of information. This attack was a three days nightmare. It stunned the Nation and virtually held it to ransom for over sixty hours. There was a stark similarity with the humiliation suffered by us in 1962. The Prime Minister had then confessed that he was living in a world divorced from reality. After 26/11, the Prime Minister apologized to the Nation. In 1962 the Defence Minister was sacked and after 26/11 the Home Minister was removed. In both these cases the total failure of the political and professional leadership stood fully exposed. The Union Cabinet was in disarray with Ministers speaking in different voice. As already mentioned, the External Affairs Minister declared that all options were open to India and the following day the Prime Minister corrected him saying that all options except war. Two Ministers opposed SIMI being declared an illegal outfit despite its proved terrorist links. One Minister wanted all Bangladeshi illegal migrants to be made Indian citizens when increasing evidence was coming of some of them having terrorist links. Our professional response left much to be desired. Despite inputs available from both foreign and our own sources that a terrorist attack on Mumbai across the sea front was in the offing, the available intelligence was neither properly analysed nor duly disseminated. No precautionary measures were taken. The attack took everyone by surprise. The NSG took over nine hours to arrive in Mumbai of all elements involved in the operation were not properly co-ordinated at the site. It took us sixty hours to eliminate ten terrorists. It was, however, very creditable that an unarmed policeman caught an armed terrorist alive. He was posthumously awarded Ashok Chakra, the Nation's highest gallantry award. A redeeming feature is that, Home Minister has Chitambram made earnest efforts to remove the lacuna in our preparedness for anti-terrorist operation.

Naxals have been carrying out spectacular strikes looting rifles from police attacking jails to rescue colleagues and release prisoners, attacking railway stations, trains, police stations and so on. It is estimated that Naxals are responsible for 80% of violence in the country. The Naxal movement has flourished and gained momentum primarily because of bad governance and the economically deprived people being receptive to their ideology. Our intelligence gathering has been abysmally poor and co-ordination of operations of Police forces of different States leaves much to be desired. In early nineteenth century, British crushed the Thugee menace which accounted for thousands killed on the highways every year, primarily due to excellent intelligence network organized by Colonel Sleeman. Similarly, it was through sound intelligence gathering that Sir Charles Tegart managed to eliminate the anarchist violence in Bengal in early twentieth century. Besides, poor leadership at the junior level of both the police and the para military, has allowed the Naxals to score repeated success inflicting heavy casualties on policemen. Police stations are the cutting edge of Police administration. They have been sorely neglected. There were some 12,000 police stations in India at the time of Independence. Our population has increased more than threefold and so have complexities of policing in modern times. Armed Police battalions at the Centre and in the Staes have increased from about 25 in 1947 to over 2,000 now. The new Home Minister is making long overdue efforts to improve the Police Stations. Significant success has been achieved in Andhra Pradesh through a combination of development activity and effective security action against armed Naxal cadres. Isolating the Naxals from the people and at the same time destroying their combat potential, are imperative to overcome the grave internal threat to national security.

To conclude, it needs to be reiterated that sound intelligence is the bedrock for success in dealing with terrorism. In the absence of good intelligence, dealing with a terrorist is like looking for a needle in a haystack. With accurate intelligence, terrorist attack can be prevented. British intelligence services to their great credit, unearthed the macabre plot of Islamists blowing up seven trans-Atlantic airliners in mid-air over the Atlantic, using liquid bombs and killing thousands of passengers. Within two years, the trial of culprits was completed and they were awarded life sentence. As for follow up action after a terrorist attack, the action taken by the US after 9/11 is a good example. Through a combination of defensive and offensive measures, it has been ensured that another terrorist attack has not taken place in that country. Another point that needs to be stressed is that the war on terror must be fought through offensive action so that the terrorist's capability gets destroyed. No war is won by only defensive action. There are four Ps which should form part of the doctrine for counter terrorist operations. First, Political Will. Hard political decisions must be taken and under no circumstance, policy of appeasement or vote bank politics should be allowed to prevail. The latter leads to a paralysis in decision making. Second, Professionalism. The intelligence agencies, security forces, administration and criminal justice system must be suitably geared to deal with this challenge, displaying high standards of professionalism. Third, People's support. People should be mobilized both for providing information and for countering terrorist propaganda. Fourth, Propaganda. The terrorist fights with two weapons namely the gun and propaganda. He has to be neutralized on both these fronts. Margaret Thatcher had rightly stated that the media provides oxygen to the terrorists. That oxygen must be denied to them.

14

LEARNING FROM DANTEWADA

The massacre of 76 Policemen at Dantewada sent shock waves throughout the country, just as the Pakistan launched terrorist attack on 26/11 in Mumbai, had done. The latter led to a change of guard in the Ministry of Home Affairs. Chidambaram injected dynamism into a somnolent Ministry. One appreciated his earnestness and various measures he initiated. For several years, the Prime Minister had been saying that Maoist terrorism was the biggest threat to the Nation, but little had been done to deal with the problem. Dantewada has highlighted gaping weaknesses in our ability to combat the Maoists. These need to be addressed urgently.

When the Nation faces a grave threat to its survival, it is imperative that we put up a united front. Just before the Kargil war, it was distressing that the then Opposition had put up an inflated rubber bus turned upside down to ridicule the Prime Minister's attempt at bus diplomacy. It is gratifying that after the Dantewada, the Opposition has closed ranks in support of the Home Minister. This is as it should be.

For the first few days, the media was parroting that a thousand Maoists had attacked the CRP Company at Dantewada. Then this number came down to 300. Initially there was no report of any Maoist getting killed but now it is being said that eight of them got killed, showing that the CRP company did put up a fight. Only one newspaper reported that Satyavan Singh Yadav, the Deputy Commandant was wounded, yet he killed a few Maoists before he was hacked to death. Such confusion in reporting does not do us any credit.

Several hundreds Police and Paramilitary personnel have got killed on account of poor leadership and poor training. In February 2004 Maoists attacked the Police armoury at Korapat in Orissa looting 500 rifles and a large quantity of ammunition. In November 2005, Maoists attacked the District Jail at Jehanabad in Bihar and released their colleagues and some 350 prisoners. Such instances taking place in broad daylight at district headquarters, without any resistance, shows complete collapse of administration. There have also been other deplorable instances. In Chattisgarh, thirty armed Policemen inside a building were killed. In a CRP post, men watching Indo-Pak cricket match on the television were killed. At Sildah in West Bengal, 24 armed men of East Frontier Rifles were killed without offering any opposition.. 36 Greyhound commandos of Andhra Police travelling relaxed in a motor launch in a lake, without taking elementary precautions, were gunned down.

Having gone through arduous three month jungle training like all other Army personnel inducted into Burma from 1943 onwards, I can vouch for the great importance ofjungle training. Vigorous jungle training must be imparted to all police and para military personnel operating against Maoists. The Army has a Jungle Warfare school at Vairangte in Mizoram. The CRP company at Dantewada had done no jungle training. Fields of fire are limited in jungles and open spaces can be death traps. At Dantewada, the CRP company walked blindly into such a killing ground covered by the Maoists. The support of the tribals in the jungles should also be mobilized. The British had raised Lushai, Kachin and Naga levies. These gave invaluable support for operations in the jungles. We can do the same for fighting Maoists. This will also assist in economic development by providing employment in the region.

Glaring deficiencies of the paramilitary in leadership at both field and supervisory levels, must be made up urgently. An executive Police officer, looking after Police Stations and other Police functioning, is as unsuited for such operations as a nimmeture Army officer for running Police administration. In 1973, I recall, we had put up a scheme for lateral induction of officers and men from combat arms to Para Military, after a certain number of years. This would solve the problem of a full career for the soldier while maintaining the Army's youthful profile and at the same time provide military expertise and experience to the Para Military. This would have also meant a saving to the exchequer of hundreds of crores in the seventies due to reduced expenditure on pension and training costs. Today this would run into thousands of crores. After nearly 40 years, the Sixth Pay Commission has made the same recommendation. Would the babudom of Delhi and the Para Military top brass, zealously guarding their turf, allow this recommendation to be implemented ?

No doubt law and order is a State subject and it is very legitimate for States to guard their autonomy on this score. Maoist terrorism is not a normal law and order problem. It is a war unleashed against the Nation. It does not respect inter State boundaries. The Centre making Para Military available to the States and expecting them to fight this war with the buck stopping at the Chief Minister, is not enough. During the Second World War, the Allies without asserting their individual sovereignty, allowed overall strategic direction of the war to be given by the Big Three – Roosevelt, Churchill and Stalin. At the theatre level, unified commands under Supreme Commanders in command of all services cutting across nationalities and international boundaries, were set up. Similarly we need a supreme body with the Union Home Minister and Chief Ministers of affected States to formulate overall policies. Under this apex body, there should be zones worked out on the basis of geographical and other considerations, ignoring inter State boundaries. In each zone there should be a unified command under a suitable-Police officer or an Army officer on deputation. All agencies within the zone - Police, Para Military and Intelligence - should report to him. At the zonal level, there should be a committee of Chief Ministers of the Zone, for giving policy directions to the Zonal Commanders. During the Second World War, sovereignty of Allied nations nor international boundaries came in the way of conduct of war. Similarly, neither the autonomy of States nor inter-State boundaries, should impinge upon the war against Maoists.

The CRP company at Dantewada was ambushed when it was returning after a three days jungle dominating patrol.

Such patrols serve little purpose. They are like a sword striking the water and are a fruitless exercise. What we need are impregnable redoubts of minimum company strength with suitable defences. There will then be no question of any Maoist attack succeeding against them. These can become bases for sending out small patrols to gather intelligence, which could be supplemented by other intelligence inputs. On that basis, surgical strikes should be carried out against Maoists. These redoubts can also be bases from which development works in the region can be organised. In 1968, I was commanding a brigade of nine battalions in the jungles of Manipur. I had 42 such air maintained posts to dominate the jungles. None of which were ever attacked by the Nagas. My flanking formation in Nagaland was also working on the same strategy. We captured gang of 300 Nagas led by Mowu Angami, the Commander-in-Chief of Naga Army returning from Yunan in China after training in modern areas and equipped with modern weapons. training and carrying new weapons.

15

COMBATING MAOIST TERRORISM

For some years the Prime Minister has been saying that Maoist violence is the biggest threat to our internal security. He reiterated this at his recent anniversary Press conference but did not indicate how he proposed to tackle the problem beyond saying that he was keeping in touch with the Chief Ministers. After 26/11, a somnolent Ministry of Home got energised. Chidambram with his dedicated approach to tackling internal security, brought a breath of fresh air, raising hopes that at long last, internal security issues will now be suitably addressed. Opposition has been fully supportive of him but within his own party, dissident voices have been raised. Prime Minister has not shown any signs of setting this right. To compound matters, unnecessary controversies have been raised about where the buck stops and about limited mandate. Having made a good beginning, setbacks at Dantawade and after, seem to have shaken the Government's resolve. The request for 72 hours of peace to start dialogue showed a state of demoralization. Not unexpectedly, the Maoists turned down the offer. They replied with a dastardly explosion at Midnapore on 28 May, resulting in 141 deaths of innocent civilians. Talks with Maoists when held, should only be from a position of strength and not of weakness.

Before examining what needs to be done, we need to have a quick look at the dimensions of Maoist problem. Through years of sustained bad governance, affected States have driven their deprived people in undeveloped regions to the arms of Maoists. The latter have declared a war against the Indian State in which thousands of innocent civilians and security personnel have been killed. We also need to have a quick look at some of the incidents of Maoist violence that have been taking place to show the ineffectiveness of Government apparatus. Such instances taking place in broad daylight at district headquarters, without any resistance, show complete collapse of administration. There have also been other deplorable instances. A prestigious train like the Rajdhani Express was hijacked in West Bengal. In Chattisgarh thirty armed Policemen relaxing in a post were mowed down. In a CRP post, men watching Indo-Pak cricket match on the television were killed. Dantewada 1 and Dantewada 2 have been a continuation of such attacks.

We have all the resources to crush Maoists, yet our record has been so dismal. We have 210 battalions of CRP. It is a two lakh strong force, the largest paramilitary force in the world. It is equipped with modern weapons but it has not developed the culture and ethos for fighting well armed hostiles. It is the most outstretched force in our country with poor logistic infrastructure. This affects its morale. Apart from being ill trained, it is very poorly led. For the first two decades after Independence, its battalion commanders would remain at Neemuch in Central India, while their companies would be engaged in operations in Kashmir or the North East. The culture of officers not leading from the front persists. State Police forces have expanded considerably, both in terms of their armed police battalions and their extremely top heavy higher rank structure, but police stations have been woefully neglected both in numbers and in resources. This has had a disastrous effect because the police station is the cutting edge of police administration. Of course, the other very debilitating factor is the politicisation of Police and their becoming the handmaiden of the ruling party in power. As for intelligence agencies, despite their proliferation, they seldom provide actionable intelligence. In all these years of Maoist violence, the only Maoist leader of consequence apprehended has been one Malla Raj Reddy. He jumped the bail in December 2009.

There is no reason why we cannot successfully wipe out the Maoist menace if we show the required will and determination to do so. Anti-Maoist operations should not be allowed to become tne plaything of party politics or fellow travellers of Maoists masquerading in the garb of intellectuals and human rights activists. We must have the right organizational structure and pursue right strategy and tactics for winning this war. In all these respect, we are in a state of total disarray.

No doubt our Constitution has made law and order a State subject. Maoist problem is not a normal law and order issue. Maoists have openly declared a war against the State. Fighting a war is the responsibility of the Centre, as laid down in our Constitution. Maoists do not respect inter State boundaries. Given these ground realities, it is absurd to follow the normal practice of providing central para military forces to State Governments and leave it to the latter to fight Maoists. It is equally absurd to quibble over whether combating the Maoist menace is a Centre or State responsibility. What is desperately required is that, both the Centre and States, unitedly and in a co-ordinated manner conduct operations to wipe out the Maoist menace. This requires a suitable command structure guiding and controlling operations. The Centre has all the powers under the Constitution and the Central Government has the required national mandate. A State Government cannot be allowed to tow a separate line in fighting this war for national survival. Similarly we need to have an apex body comprising the Union Home Minister and Chief Ministers of affected States with unified zonal commands to conduct the war against Maoists without being hampered by considerations of State autonomy or State boundaries. The apex body at the Centre should have a highly competent and experienced Security Adviser. The latter may be a serving or retired officer and he should be from the Army or Police, preferably the latter. Maoist affected areas should be carved into zones on the basis of geographical and other considerations without worrying too much about State boundaries. A committee of Chief Ministers of the affected States should give policy directions but the conduct of operations should be left to a Zonal Commander of the rank of DGP. If a suitable Police officer is not available, then an Army officer on deputation should be chosen for this appointment. All the resources of the State in a zone should be made available to the Zonal Commander. The paramilitary, the police, intelligence, publicity and development work in militancy affected areas in the Zone, should be co-ordinated by him. Zones may be divided into sub-zones, as necessary, where Sub-Zonal Commanders may function on the same lines.

The strategy to be adopted should be based on our national aim, which should be to inflict heaviest possible attrition on Maoists and liberate tribals, from being exploited or terrorized by Maoists. While doing so, minimum possible collateral damage should be caused and human rights duly respected. Based on this broad approach, a three prong strategy of intensified operations, economic development and public relations should be pursued. Some people argue that economic development should be given priority over security operations. There are others who maintain that successful security operations are a pre-requisite for any development activity. Maoists have been attacking schools, hospitals, communication towers, roads and so on. How can any development activity be conducted in such areas without a modicum of security ? Without getting into the chicken or the egg arriving first argument, we should accept that both operations and development are important. As far as possible, both need to be conducted simultaneously. Even if development activities in certain areas may be difficult on account of security considerations, some development effort in terms of poverty alleviation for those areas can be conducted. Jobs for locals outside the affected areas can be arranged in Government service or in corporate sector, after necessary training. Small children from these areas can be provided free quality education and boarding in a city at par with education imparted in leading public schools. A NGO in Bihar has been working on such a scheme in Patna for the poorest of the poor children in villages and this has been a great success. Every effort should be made to ensure that the produce of tribals brought to marks get a good price and locals not allowed to suffer at hands of mining or land mafias. Other innovative measures benefiting these people can also be undertaken till security scenario is made conducive for undertaking development work inside these Maoist dominated areas. Third prong of the strategy of maintaining good public image through suitable publicity and appropriate approach is very important in our present information age.

Tactical plans should take into account tactics of Maoists. They have been carrying out well prepared hit and run attacks on soft targets to terrorise and demoralise the people. They are not bothered if in the process they kill hundreds of innocent civilians. Untrained and badly led para military forces, often failing to comply with tactical requirements, have been attacked repeatedly and have suffered heavy casualties. There has been no instance of a pitched battle between security forces and Maoists. The latter are dominating large areas of forests where there is no presence of security forces. Two immediate requirements have to be met to enable the CRP to take on Maoists. First, the Army should run special courses with emphasis on jungle warfare for all CRP units participating in anti-Maoist operations. No untrained unit should be deployed for these operations. Second, the quality of leadership should be improved on priority and those found not suitable be weeded out. Unit commanders play a key role. They must be chosen very carefully. Induction of serving Army personnel on deputation or reemployment of some young retired suitable army personnel should be considered. Lateral transfer of officers and men in their early or mid thirties from combat arms to para military was taken up by the Army in 1972. The Sixth Pay Commission has also made this recommendation. This may be a long term measure but we should begin implementing it without further delay.

Realistic plans for operations on the ground have to be made. Maoists have a choice of unlimited soft targets and they can spring surprises. We must provide maximum possible defence for all soft targets by suitable force deployment and effective intelligence cover. It is not just possible to provide static protection for all possible targets. Priorities have to be worked out. Quick reaction teams suitably deployed should be ready to strike back immediately. All this only can minimise the damage but cannot ensure victory in this only war. As in all wars, final victory can be achieved only through offensive action like the defenced stalingred. Encounters should be sought with Maoists and heavy attrition inflicted. Their dominance of remote jungles can be removed by establishing company level, air maintained, redoubts at suitable places in remote jungles. These should be made impregnable with mines and obstacles round them. These redoubts can be the base for offensive operations in their area and focal points for organizing developmental activities. As the situation improves, civil administration should get established in their neighbouring areas.

Using the Army and Air Force for these operations is being widely debated. Army is fully stretched dealing with external threats and secessionist movements. It should not get embroiled in the war against Maoists. However, the Army can certainly give assistance in terms of training, advice and sparing few personnel on deputation. As for the Air Force, offensive operations should be avoided except in extreme emergency. We have never used offensive air power against militants in Kashmir for all these years. This causes indiscriminate casualties resulting in much suffering of innocent civilians. It will be counterproductive. There has been a lone instance of using offensive air power against militants in our country. That was at Aizauel in Mizoram. We had to use the Air Force in this role in 1966. This was done when Mizo rebellion erupted suddenly. The Government Treasury and the Police armoury at Aizawl was looted. Assam Rifles post was surrounded and was on the verge of being overwhelmed. Failure to take immediate effective action could have led to the fall of State capital to the rebels. Government took the right decision to use air power and saved the situation. Aizawl like situation is not likely to arise again. This does not mean that this option should be completely ruled out. Depending on the gravity of the situation, it should be left to the Government to decide. Logistic support in terms of air supply to air maintained posts or casualty evacuation is a different matter. Civil air resources can be mobilized for these as has been happening in the North East. Air Force could supplement this.

The present ratio of casualties being suffered in anti-Maoist operations is heavily weighted against the security forces and innocent civilians. Maoists suffer very negligible casualties. Thousands of security force personnel and innocent civilians have been killed by Maoists, while the latter have largely managed to get away with hardly any casualties. This situation cannot be allowed to continue. It has to be changed radically. In Jammu and Kashmir the number of terrorists killed every year has been almost double the combined casualties suffered by `the Security Forces and the civilians. For every soldier getting killed six to seven terrorists are being killed in encounters. Officers have been leading their men from the front. This is duly reflected in the high percentage of officer casualties. Officers are less than 3% of the strength of the Army, yet on an average over 8% of the casualties suffered by the Army, is in the officer cadre. These statistics pertaining to casualties in Kashmir have been mentioned, so that they be emulated and even improved upon in the war against Maoists.

The suggestions on command structure, strategy and tactics if implemented can without question, shatter the dreams of the Maoists to repeat what Mao had succeeded in doing against Chiang kai Siek. Indian State must use all its capability to wipe out Maoists. We can then only remove this greatest threat to our internal security repeatedly reiterated by the Prime Minister for the last six years. The Opposition and entire nation must stand up united in support of the Government, in this fight for national survival.

PART-IV
MISCELLANY

16

THE OFFICE OF GOVERNOR

Recent landmark judgment of the Supreme Court on removal of Governors should have a far reaching effect on the functioning of our democracy. Supreme Court judgment on the Keshvanand Bharati case put an end to the era of arbitrary dismissal of State Governments. Hopefully, the arbitrary removal of Governors, which has been resorted to so frequently, will now become a thing of the past. Indira Gandhi patronised the concept of committed judiciary, committed Governors and committed civil servants. Fortunately, the judiciary asserted its independence and now Governors should be able to function independently. A neutral civil service remains a far cry at present.

We may trace the origin of office of Governor in India. Initially the East India Company ruled over its newly acquired territory through the Presidency Governors of Bengal, Madras and Bombay. Later in 1773, a Governor General was superimposed over them as the supreme authority in India. The Hindi word Lat for Governor in popular parlance stood for ultimate authority. A common rebuke was that you are not a Lat. The British had three grades of Lats - Mulki Lat (Viceroy), Suba Lat (provincial Governors) and Jangi Lat (Commander-in-Chief). The former was supreme. Other Lats reported to him and took orders. All Lats were addressed as Your Excellency. Before dufling to by then, they lived in regal splendor – the Viceroy in Viceregal Lodge Simla, the Governors in Lal Mahal and the Commander in Chief, Jutog, Simla. They flew the Union Jack on their cars. The Viceroy and the Governors held

Durbars in Mughal style and also investitures to award titles and medals. They enjoyed the acme of power and splendor. It was said that the King of England reigned but not ruled; the President of America ruled but not reigned. The Viceroy of India both reigned and ruled.

With the dawn of Independence, the old order changed drastically. The President at Centre and Governors in the States became constitutional heads and shed their executive powers. Prime Minister and Chief Ministers became the repository of executive power. Yet the President and the Governors retained some of the regal trappings of yore. As for the Jangi Lat or the Commander-in-Chief, that institution has vanished. That designation has gone to the President. His successors, three Sevice Chiefs, are not even his pale shadow. In a perverted interpretation of the concept of supremacy of the civil, they were subordinated to civil servants in both functioning and protocol. They were isolated from the process of decision making on Defence matters.

There are many who feel that the office of Governor is redundant, a useless relic of the past. Even during the deliberations of the Constituent Assembly there were a few who felt the same. Biswanath Das spoke, "You are going to have a democracy from toe to neck and autocracy at the head". The Constitution prescribes an important role for a Governor. He has to act on the advice of his council of ministers but has to use his discretion in selecting a Chief Minister. During President's rule, he has to take over governance of the State. Besides, he also has a very important role in the sphere of higher education as Chancellor of Universities. There are other constructive roles that he can perform.

The Constitution prescribes that a Governor must be a citizen of India and be over 35 years of age. The founding fathers attached great importance to the calibre of persons selected to be Governors. Alladi Krishnaswamy Iyer's view was that "a Governor should be a person of undoubted ability in public life who at the same time has not been mixed up in provincial party struggle and factions". TT Krishnachari opined that a Governor "should hold the scales impartially as between the various factions in the politics of the State". Nehru preferred eminent educationists or eminent in other walks of life, "who have not taken too great part in politics". The above ideals were given a go by long ago. Politicians have been playing musical chairs with the office of Governor. They have been Governor one day, a Chief Minister or Minister on the other day and vice versa. This puts a question mark on the political neutrality of such Governors.

Governor is appointed by the Centre but is not its agent. A wrong perception of his being so has gained currency mainly on account of many Governors acting in a blatantly biased manner. A Governor is constitutional authority under the president who derives his powers from the Constitution. He should be carrying out his duties like a judge on the basis of his own judgment and in accordance with the provisions of the Constitution. He is not required to act on directions from the Centre.

In 1946, Sir Frederick Burrows, the Governor of Bengal, asked Mahatma Gandhi that with a popular government in power what was a governor expected to do. The Mahatma replied: "Noting", This advice given to a British Governor who wielded considerable executive authority underscored the fact that even in those days, a Governor was not expected to interfere with the functioning of a popular government.

After Independence, there was a strong opinion against continuing the institution of Governor. While accepting to retain the office of Governor, Constituent Assembly ensured that did not happen. Constitution clearly defines the Governor's role. On all matters, he shall act on the advice of council of ministers except when selecting a Chief Minister.

He can recommend President's rule in special circumstances and in that event, temporarily govern the state. A section of opinion in the country now feels that the Governor is an unnecessary relic of the Raj and we could do without this institution. I feel that besides his role defined in the Constitution, a Governor has other useful roles. He is State symbol above the cut and thrust of politics. It is for nothing that in his address he uses the term 'My Government'. He should equally well use the term, 'My Opposition'. He should endeavour to earn the confidence of both. He should advice and caution the Chief Minister away from public glare.

During discussion in the Constituent Assembly, the caliber of the individual to be appointed Governor and his political impartiality were discussed at length.

The emphasis by everyone was on the political impartiality of the Governor. Unfortunately, in practice, this requirement has often been ignored. Active politicians from the ruling party are often appointed Governor. This tends to undermine the impartial image of a Governor.

With different parties ruling at the Centre and in States, role of Governors has become crucial. They are appointed on the basis of their proximity to the ruling party and at times against opposition from the State Government, as happened in the case of Dharam Veera in West Bengal or Nityanand Kanungo in Bihar. They are often the instrument of an authoritative centre to curb the autonomy of the State. The role of Governors in imposing President's rule has been notoriously partisan. However, there have been exceptions. BK Nehru as Governor of Kashmir refused to dismiss Farooq Abdulla's Government. He was transferred to Gujrat. Surjeet Singh Barnala refused to recommend dismissal of Karunannidhi Government in Tamil Nadu. He resigned. Generally, Governors have been like Ram Lal. From Chief Minister in Himachal, he was sent to Andhra Pradesh to dismiss the NT Rama Rao's government at the bidding of the Centre.

Nehru set a bad precedent by sending Justice Fazle Ali as Governor of Assam. Judges on retirement being appointed Governors has since become a common practice. This can compromise the independence of the judiciary. Similarly, former Chief Election Commissioner Ramadevi being appointed Governor of Himachal and then Karnataka, was not a good precedent.

Sarkaria Commission pointed out that out of 298 Governors appointed between 1967 and 1986, only 18 could complete their full five year term. Governors have been removed for unconvincing reasons. Justice M Fatma Beevi as Governor of Tamil Nadu asked to send a report on the Karunannidhi incident, sent a report on the same lines as State Government. Veteran Congressman and a Bharat Ratna, Subramaniam made an indiscreet remark as Governor of Maharashtra.

Both these Governors were removed. The Janata Government dismissed all Congress appointed Governors in 1977 and the Congress Government did a repeat in 1980 in the case of Janata appointed Governors. In 2004 UPA Government removed four NDA appointed Governors. I was high up on the list to be removed, with my chief Minister deparately trying to get me out, but somehow I escaped the guillotine. Given these facts, the recent judgment of the apex court on this issue provides a breath of fresh air. Insecurity of tenure of Governors has been a major cause for malfunctioning. The judgment clarifies the air on this score. To improve matters further, we also need to have transparency in the selection process of Governors. The individuals selected for this high office should be as visualised by the founding fathers of our Constitution.

In this theatre of the absurd, PDP Ministers who had processed this case for three years recommending it to the Cabinet and had been a partly to the Cabinet decision to divert the land of the Shrine Board joined this agitation. Mufti and his party went full blast to support this agitation. To appease the agitators, the government cancelled the Baltal land transfer and even dissolved the Amarnath Shrine Board. This led to three months of counter-agitation in Jammu. Ultimately, the government was forced to restore status quo ante.

The Valley Press, as usual, played a very negative role carrying out totally false and mischievous propaganda. The national secular media showed little awareness of the problem. It stated that I, as the Governor of Jammu and Kashmir, has transferred the land on the eve of my departure and set the Valley on fire when I had northing to do with that Cabinet decision beyond approving the application of the Board three years earlier.

As for the constitutional crisis involving Karnataka Governor HR. Bhardwaj, I had occasion to interact with him when he was the Union Law Minister and I found him helpful. However, his handling of the Quattrochi Scandal in regards to defreezing his London Bank account and letting him off the hook in Argentina shocked the right-thinking people.

A similar development has now taken place in Karnataka. A Congress MLC complained to the Governor against three

Cabinet Ministers. Instead of forwarding the complaint to the Speaker, Lok Ayukta, Election Commission or Chief Minister, for taking suitable action, he issued show-cause notice to the Cabinet Ministers and asked them to appear before him. For the first time in the history of Indian democracy, a Governor has taken such an unconstitutional step.

As the Ministers declined to appear before him, he forwarded the complaint to the Election Commission. He has now been publicly insisting that the Ministers be dropped from Cabinet and CBI should investigate the case. He even came lobbying to Delhi in full media glare and met the President, the Prime Minister and the Home Minister. It is the Chief Minister's prerogative to drop ministers from the Cabinet.

The Constitution provides for the Governor to recommend dismissal of the government but not of individual ministers. A Governor has the right to caution and advise a Chief Minister but this should not be done publicly. There have been numerous cases of ministers at the Centre and in the states being involved in corruption but has any President or Governor publicly asserted that the Minister concerned be dropped?

On the face of it, a major violation of the Constitution in letter and spirit appears to be taking place in Karnataka.

17

GOVERNORS AND CHIEF MINISTERS

The confrontation in Karnatak between Governor Bhardwaj, a known Congress loyalist and the BJP led Government of Yaddyurappa has raised many eyebrows. On the complaint of a Congress MLC, the Governor issued show cause notice to three Cabinet Ministers. The Union Law Minister has supported this action. The Ministers refused to appear before the Governor. The Chief Minister has taken strong objection to such intervention by the Governor. In the past, such cases were referred to the Chief Minister or to the Speaker and the Governor did not take it upon himself to carry out the investigation. Bhardwaj referred the case to the Election Commission. Naveen Chawla, another known Congress loyalist has asked for explanation from the Chief Minister through the Governor. Normally such explanations are sought directly without bringing the Governor in the loop. One does not know what the outcome of all this will be.

As Governor for eleven continuous years in Assam and Jammu and Kashmir, I tried to scrupulously follow the role prescribed for a Governor. I was however pro-active in guarding India's integrity without interfering in the functioning of the State Government. Yet I got involved in controversies with two out of the four Chief Ministers, I worked with. It will be relevant to recount this.

When I was Governor in Assam, the CBI sought my sanction

to prosecute the Chief Minister, Prafulla Kumar Mahanta. I went through the CBI's voluminous investigation report with a tooth comb and found that the CBI had failed to establish a prima facie case. I sent for Director CBI and apprised him of my views. I told him that if further evidence was produced I could revise my opinion. He could not send me any additional evidence. I rejected the recommendation of the CBI. This was the first time that a Governor had rejected the recommendation of the country's premier investigation agency. This became a major national controversy. The Congress party MPs from Assam petitioned the President to recall me. A PIL was filed in the High Court. It upheld my decision.

The second controversy pertained to my 42 paged printed report on illegal migration from Bangladesh to the President with copy to the Prime Minister and the Chief Minister. I consulted the Chief Minister. He fully agreed with me but could not do anything about it due to compulsions of coalition politics. The problem had become more acute over the years. It had led to the eruption of militancy in the State. My report highlighted that the unabated influx from Bangladesh not only threatened the demography of Assam but also the Nation's security. I recommended that the IMDT Act which was designed to facilitate illegal migration and which applied to Assam only and not to other States, be scrapped. My report was serialized in full in all the newspapers of Assam. It took Assam by storm. Many Congress leaders meeting me in private applauded me for what I had done but said that for political reasons they had to oppose my report. They again petitioned the President for my recall. When the Congress came to power in Assam, I had to read my address to the Assembly which stated that there was no illegal migration into Assam and the IMDT Act was necessary to maintain communal harmony. This created an uproar all over the State. People accused me of shameless volte face and the Press was highly critical of me. I had a Press communiqué issued saying that the Governor's address reflected the views of the State Government and not of the Governor. Tarun Gogoi told the Press that I had committed a grave constitutional impropriety and he would be taking up the matter with the Centre. Nothing came out of it. A PIL was filed in the Supreme Court. The apex court struck down the obnoxious IMDT Act quoting extensively from my report to the

President. This vindicated my stand.

I had very good relations with Prafulla Kumar Mahanta in Assam and Ghulam Nabi Azad in Kashmir. Together we achieved much. Due to my personal contacts with the Army, which had a large presence in both these States, I was able to get a tremendous lot done by it both in combating militancy and in initiatives to win the hearts and minds of the people. I had differences with Tarun Gogoi on illegal migration issue but otherwise, our relations were good. Unfortunately, my relations with Mufti Mohammad Sayeed were far from cordial. He had a marked communal outlook and a strong bias in favour of the separatists. He wanted healing touch for the terrorists rather than for the victims of terrorists. He succeeded in getting Government pension for families of terrorists killed in encounter with security forces. Such a bizarre arrangement does not obtain anywhere in the world. It virtually provides a fillip to terrorism. He was opposed to improving the horrible living conditions of Kashmiri Pandits in refugee camps around Jammu. Much to his chagrin, I managed to get Manmohan Singh to rectify this. He was opposed to extending the duration of Amarnath Yatra and improving facilities for the pilgrims. The High Court overruled him. He wanted dual currency in Kashmir and a united Upper House with Pakistan in the State Legislature, and so on. In 2004 when the UPA Government came to power he tried desperately to get me removed along with the four other BJP appointed Governors. The Press was full of speculation for one month. He failed in his attempt. This only made matters worse. Despite our differences, I tried to show a façade of amity with him. After his term as Chief Minister expired and the Congress got its turn, he became more bitter and created difficulties not only for me but also for his successor and coalition partner, Ghulam Nabi Azad.

Harmonious relations between a Governor and a Chief Minister are in the interest of the State. The Governor should show no political bias nor interfere with governance in the State. He should be friendly with the Chief Minister and be available for advice whenever necersary. At the same time Governor should earn confidence of the Opposition. A public controversy between the Governor and the Chief Minister only undermines the dignity of both these high offices.

18

AGONY OF A SOFT STATE

We take legitimate pride in the fact that through thousands of years of our history, we have never embarked on an invasion of any foreign country. However, what is not so flattering is that we neglected our national security, particularly in the medieval and modern periods. This resulted in our succumbing to invasions and suffering prolonged subjugation. Since Independence, we have managed to keep our borders inviolate and defeated conventional military invasions, except in 1962 when we faltered. However, our record of dealing with terrorism unleashed against us from across our borders, has been dismal. No wonder we are viewed as a soft State by the world.

Israel's prompt and often overwhelming response to terrorist attacks has kept its enemies at bay. USA sent its forces across oceans and continents in retaliation for the dastardly terrorist attack of 9/11. We did not send our forces even a few thousand yards beyond the LOC to attack terrorist camps in territory claimed by us and in illegal occupation of Pakistan. We reconciled ourselves to being at the receiving end of the strategy of thousand cuts. The terror attack in Mumbai on 26/11 exposed numerous chinks in our armour. The Union Cabinet was in complete disarray over dealing with terrorism. The Foreign Minister reacted soon after saying that all options were open to India. The following day, the Prime Minister corrected him and said that all options but war were open. Two Ministers were trying to defend SIMI. One Minister was wanting all Bangladeshi illegal migrants to be made Indian citizens. Another Minister wanted judicial inquiry into the Batla terrorist incident, implying that it could be a faked encounter staged by the Police. He also wanted Government funds utilized to defend the students accused in that terrorist attack. Yet another Minister insinuated that Hemant Karkare was killed by Hindu extremists. That was not all. The Minister representing India at the UN forgot to mention that Jews had been massacred at Nariman House in Mumbai. The Prime Minister now ruled out any retaliatory action beyond repeatedly asserting that there will be no dialogue with Pakistan till the culprits of the Mumbai attack are booked. A few weeks before his surrender at Sharm el Sheikh, he had talked tough with Zardari about his mandate being restricted to talking about terrorism emanating from Pakistan. However, in the meeting in Egypt with the Pakistan Prime Minister, he meekly agreed to Pakistani demand for delinking talks with terrorism. He followed in the footsteps of Chamberlain at Munich, wanting peace at all costs. He even outdid Chamberlain by causing self-inflicted wound on his own country. Where was the need to mention Baluchistan in the joint statement? Pakistan may have been accusing India of complicity with insurgents in Baluchistan but no one ever paid any credence to that. There is no geographical contiguity between India and Baluchistan. Unlike several hundred Pakistani terrorists caught in Kashmir, not one Indian has been found in Baluchistan. India has refrained from taking advantage of the situation in Northern Areas where the people are reeling under Pakistani oppression, notwithstanding some leaders from Northern Areas seeking Indian assistance. Pakistan is today gloating over the inclusion of Baluchistan in the joint statement. Doubts have been created in the minds of the international community about India's involvement in Baluchistan, by virtue of India agreeing to include Baluchistan in the joint statement. At Havana the Prime Minister accepted that Pakistan, the epicentre of international terrorism, be equated with India as a co-victim of terrorism and the two should carry out joint investigation. At Sharm-el-Sheikh he has now vityually conceded by implication that India, the innocent victim of terrorism, being portrayed as an aggressor.

In trying to defend the indefensible, the spin doctors have

been coming out with bizarre justifications. The blame is being laid on the bureaucracy for bad drafting. The buck cannot and should not stop there. The person approving the draft must bear the responsibility. It is also being said that the joint statement is not a legal document and is therefore not binding. This only exposes us as a nation to ridicule. How can a joint statement agreed to by our Prime Minister be dismissed so lightly? We are also told that our Prime Minister took a bold decision as Finance Minister when he introduced liberalization and in his first term when he struck the nuclear deal and now in Egypt he has again done so to usher peace on the sub-continent. The less said about such lame justifications the better.

The recent end-user monitoring agreement with the US is a grave assault on the Nation's sovereignty and self respect. Pakistan is desperately dependent on American aid for survival and has been receiving billions as aid. It successfully resisted US pressure to monitor utilization of that aid. The USA was forced to give in and the monitoring clause was dropped. Being a soft State, India could not resist US pressure and agreed to a humiliating end-user monitoring arrangement.

After the Indo-US nuclear agreement, Prime Minister announced that people of India love George Bush. In the eighteenth century, Indian rulers entered into Subsidiary Alliance with the British forfeiting their independence. Let us hope that in the twenty first century, India is not led into a Subsidiary Alliance with USA compromising her national sovereignty.

19

MISUSE OF AWARDS

It has been a well established tradition for a State to confer awards and titles on its citizens. The peers in Britain have hereditary titles but recently life peers have been introduced there. Peers are in five grades - Duke, Earl, Marquis, Viscount and Baron. Lord Sinha was the only Indian before Independence to be made a peer. After 1947 a few Indians have been made Barons. Knights rank below peers. Many Indians were knighted during the British era. Rabindranath Tagore was the first Indian Nobel Laureate. He was made a knight. Later, he returned his knighthood in protest against the Jalianwala bag massacre. There was also the Indian award of Kaiser-e-Hind, which was awarded for distinguished service. Mahatma Gandhi received this award for his service in the Boer War. He returned this award in 1920, when he started the civil disobedience movement.

British have also awards of different orders, each having grades. These orders are, Order of Bath, Queen Victoria Order, Order of St Michael and George, Order of the British Empire, Order of the Star of India and the Order of the Indian Empire. After India became independent, the latter two orders were closed. These orders have gradations like Grand Knight Commander, Knight Commander and Companion. The order of British Empire has five grades – GBE, KBE, CBE, OBE and MBE. Below these British awards were Indian awards of Rai Bahadur for Hindus, Sikhs, Khan, Bahadur for Muslims and Sardar Bahadur for Sikhs and similarly Rai Saheb, Khan Saheb and Sardar Saheb.

During the struggle for Independence, Congress felt that awards promoted toadyism among the people. It called for a boycott of titles and awards. However, honorifics got attached to the names of some of our great leaders. Rabindranath Tagore called Gandhiji, Mahatma and this caught on. Gandhiji called Vallabhbhai Patel, Sardar and Rajendra Prasad, Desh Ratna. Similarly CR Das came to be known as Deshbandhu. After Independence, Jayaprakash Narayan acquired the honorific of Loknayak and Gopi Nath Bordoloi, Lokpriya.

On attaining Independence, we initially decided not to have any titles or awards other than for gallantry. USA and France have only gallantry awards. After the Kashmir War, we introduced gallantry awards, the Vir Chakra series in war and Ashok Chakra series in peace, corresponding to such awards during the British era. In 1954 awards were introduced for distinguished service like Padma series for civilians and Vishist Seva series for military personnel. The Padma series has four grades Bharat Ratna, Padma Vibhushan, Padma Bhushan and Padma Sri. These awards are also related to the status of the individual and to the level of his attainments. The Vishist Seva series for the military has three grades of Param Vishisht Seva Medal, Ati Vishisht Seva Medal and Vishisht Sewa Medal. In exceptional cases, military personnel are also given Padma awards. Manekshaw was made a Field Marshal and also given the Padma Vibhushan, the second highest civilian award. Arthur Wellesley the first British Field Marshal got the highest civil award of his country and became the Duke of Wellington. On that analogy, Manekshaw should have been given a Bharat Ratna for India's unique military victory in thousands of years of her history. On becoming Prime Minister, Morarji Desai abolished the Padma series of awards but these got revived after him.

There has been criticism that these national awards are given on the basis of an individual's acceptability to the ruling establishment. Many deserving individuals get overlooked because of the bias against them of those in authority. On the basis of his unparalleled achievement, Sardar Patel should have been among the first to be awarded the Bharat Ratna. However, this award was given to him fifty years after his death! He got this along with Rajiv Gandhi but his name appeared after Rajiv Gandhi. All Congress Prime Ministers received Bharat

Ratna except Narsimha Rao, despite his great contribution in liberalsing the economy. Possibly, political considerations related to Babri Masjid or his involvement in scams, came in his way. Maulana Azad set a fine example by refusing to accept Bharat Ratna, as he had been a member of the award committee. This was later given to him posthumously. When I was Governor of Assam, I pleaded with President Narayanan and Prime Ministers Gujral and Vajpayee for a Bharat Ratna for Gopinath Bordoloi. He was the first Chief Minister of Assam and had saved Assam from becoming a part of East Pakistan. He had also been the architect of the Sixth Schedule of the Constitution. I had to struggle against the decision taken lately, not to give these awards posthumously. Moreover there were demands for Bharat Ratna for Biju Patnaik and NT Rama Rao. However we succeeded in getting this award for Bordoloi nearly fifty years after his death. Apart from the fact that he eminently deserved this award, I had a special reason for sponsoring his case. The people of Assam felt neglected and discriminated. This had been the main cause of insurgency in the State. The award to Bordoloi had an electrifying effect all over Assam. It helped us to win the hearts and minds of the people and get them back into the national mainstream. Similarly in Kashmir, we got a Padma Bhushan for Mian Bashir, the oldest Bakherwal political leader in the State, much revered by his community. Gujjars and Bakherwals constitute 20 per cent of the population of Jammu and Kashmir. They are backward tribes who nurture a feeling of deprivation. This award had a healthy impact. I may add that the award of Padma Vibhushan to Atal Beharee Vajpayee in 1992 by a Congress Government set a healthy tradition.

The 2010 awards of Padma Bhushan to a hotelier with a criminal background and a Padma Shri to a former militant with a dubious record, have generated much controversy. This has devalued these awards. We need to either abolish awards altogether or introduce a fair and transparent system of selection which inspires confidence. An awards committee comprising representatives of the ruling party and the Opposition plus some eminent apolitical citizens should be constituted to screen recommendations for awards. Service to the Nation and not to the party in power should be the criterion for selection.

20

THE JINNAH CONTROVERSY

Facts of history going back to over half a century are best left to historians and research scholars to unravel and interpret. A politician attempting to do so will inevitably become suspect. He will be accused of trying to draw political mileage from it.

Whisky sipping, ham eating, brilliant barrister Jinnah always dressed impeccably in Saville Row suits. He had a Parsi wife and was far removed from religious fundamentalism. His mentor in politics was the great nationalist, Dadabhai Nowrojee. His secular credentials in his early life cannot be questioned. After the Lucknow Pact of 1915, he was hailed as an ambassador of Hindu Muslim unity. Even so, there was a fly in the ointment in that pact. Whereas weightage of 25% for Muslims in excess of their numbers was understandable, insistence on preserving separate electorate promoted separatism, leading to the partition of the country.

Jinnah's boast that he created Pakistan with the help of his typewriter was not far wrong. He championed the two nation theory to the hilt and had his way, albeit not fully. He had to accept the concurrent partition of Bengal and Punjab. In his own words, he achieved a moth eaten Pakistan. After becoming Governor Genral of Pakistan he went to Iran and told the King that he has taken one third of India as Pakistan. The latter scolded him saying: he should have wanted till there were more than half Muslims and would how get half of India. Speaking with the benefit of hindsight, one can say that if Jinnah had been less obdurate and Congress more accommodative,

Partition need not have taken place. The holocaust that occurred in its wake with millions killed and millions uprooted, could have been avoided. On 29 July 1946 Jinnah announced his Direct Action plan at the Muslim League Council declaring, "Today we bid good bye to constitutional means. We have also forged a pistol and are in a position to use it." Kolkata and Noakhali under Suhrawardy killings started a cycle of violence which spread like a wild fire from one end of the country to the other.

Much is made of Jinnah's inaugural address to the Pakistan Constituent Assembly on 11 August 1947. "We are starting with the fundamental principle that we are all citizens of one State. Now I think we should keep that in front of us as an ideal and you will find that in course of time Hindus would not be Hindus, Muslims would cease to be Muslims not in the religious sense because that is the personal faith of each individual but in the political sense, as citizens of the State". This raised hopes that the arch priest of the two nation theory had gone back to his secular moorings of his young days. This hope was belied by subsequent disclosure and events. Dr Kripal Singh in his book, Select Documents on Partition, has made an interesting disclosure. Lord Ismay the Chief of Staff of Mountbatten in 1947, told Dr Singh in an interview on 17 August 1964 the background to that inaugural address. Mountbatten had asked him to convey to Jinnah the need for his taking that line, now that he had achieved his Pakistan. The sole aim for this was to check the spiraling violence in Punjab. Jinnah's address to the Karachi Bar Association on 25 January 1948 reflected his true thinking. "Why this feeling of nervousness that the future Constitution of Pakistan is going to be in conflict with Shariat laws? Islamic principles are as applicable to life as they were 1300 years ago. Islam is not only a set of rituals, traditions and spiritual doctrines. Islam is a code for every Muslim which regulates his life and conduct in even politics and economics and the like". Sir Syed Ahmed, the initial propounder of the two nation theory had stated on 16 March 1888, "is it possible that the two nations – the Mohammedans and the Hindus – would sit on the same throne and remain equal in power? Most certainly not. It is necessary that one of them should conquer the other. Then our Mussalman bothers, the Pathans will come out as a swarm of locusts from their mountain valley and make rivers of blood flow from their frontier in the North to the extreme end in Bengal." In line with this thinking, Jinnah unleashed the tribal raiders led by Pakistan Army in Kashmir. His dream got thwarted on the outskirts of Srinagar in the battle of Shelatang on 7 November 1947. The Jinnah of 1946 had thundered that he would have India divided or India destroyed. Perhaps his thinking after attaining his cherished objective had changed. He now wanted India both divided and destroyed.

Some apologists of Jinnah have been trying to project the line that Nehru and Patel were equally responsible for partition. This is mischievous. Nehru and Patel were throughout opposed to the two nation theory. Nehru not accommodating the Muslim League in the UP Cabinet in 1937 or his statement in Mumbai in 1946 that the Congress would enter the Constituent Assembly unfettered by any limitation, may have been in conformity with democratic practice but in the event, precipitated Partition. Being a pragmatist, Patel realized in 1947 that there was no alternative to Partition. After his experience in a coalition government with the Muslim League and with communal violence in the country spinning out of control, Patel realized that the country was heading towards civil war. To compound matters, the Army which in 1946 had remained strictly impartial, by mid 1947 started showing signs of being bitten by the communal virus. Prolonged deployment in such operations particularly in Punjab from where the bulk of the soldiers came and where their families were becoming victims of communal violence, was bound to affect their impartiality. At that time, the civil administration in Punjab had collapsed. The Army was the only effective instrument available to the Government to maintain order. If Partition was not accepted, the country's descent to civil war with the Army on communal basis participating from both sides, could not be prevented. India might have broken up like Yugoslavia or could have emerged like Lebanon suffering endless conflict. Moreover a patchwork unity with a weak centre would not have been conducive to the successful integration of the Princely States. In the circumstance Patel's decision to salvage 80 per cent of the country and accept Partition was an act of great statesmanship. Nehru agreed to this. Had this not been done, a united India today with a 40 per cent minority susceptible to petro dollar funded Islamist fundamentalism, would have been in a chaotic state.

Neither deifying nor demonizing Jinnah for political reasons helps us today. Let us bury the controversy and not allow it to become a bone of contention in the politics of the country. Jinnah must be turning in his grave to see what the politics of the two nation theory and of communal violence, has done to the country he created.

21

SUPREMACY OF CIVIL POWER

All the instruments of the State in a democracy function under an elected government. The supremacy of the civil over the military took time to get fully established. One day during the American Civil War, Abraham Lincoln went to the house of General McCellan, Commander of the Union Army. The General sent word that he would meet him in his office. Lincoln was asked how he tolerated such insolence. He replied that he would hold the stirrup of McCellan's horse for the sake of victory in war. Later, Lincoln dismissed him for his military failure and replaced him with General Grant. Bismarck was the architect of the military victories of Prussia. During the Franco-Prussian war, a correspondent of The Times asked the Chancellor as to how far the Prussian Army was from Paris. He replied that he knew no more about that than the correspondent. General Von Moltke used to send his war despatches only to the Emperor. In Britain, the Duke of Cambridge, a cousin of Queen Victoria was the Commander-in-Chief of the Army for thirty years. During that period no Prime Minister could interfere with the functioning of the Army.

Supremacy of the civil over the military got fully established in the twentieth century. Curzon Kitchener dispute in India was something different. Kitchener did not question the supremacy of Curzon but wanted more power for himself and a more rational working arrangement. Curzon strongly opposed this. Kitchener with his links in London, managed to have his way. Curzon resigned. Two incidents pertaining to the conduct of war during the First World War are of much significance. Churchill was the Minister for the Navy and Lord Fisher was the Naval Chief. Churchill wanted the Navy to launch an operation through the Dardanelles to knock Turkey out of the war. Fisher remonstrated with Churchill advising against such a hazardous operation. Churchill overruled Fisher. He expounded his plan at a Cabinet meeting. Fisher was in attendance but kept silent. He felt it would be disloyal for him to oppose his Minister. The Cabinet construed Fisher's silence as his concurrence and sanctioned the operation. Dardanelles operation became the greatest disaster in the history of the Royal Navy. The Parliamentary Committee inquiring into this fiasco indicted both Fisher and Churchill. Fisher was dismissed and Churchill had to go into political oblivion. Later Churchill bounced back and in the Second World War proved to be the greatest war leader of his country. The second instance pertained to Prime Minister Lloyd George and the Army Chief, General Robertson. Lloyd George felt that the first world war had been fought to a standstill in the trenches of France. He wanted some divisions to be diverted from France to the East for operations against Turkey. Robertson was opposed to this as he felt that France was the main theatre, where the war had to be fought and won. For the French, the war in France was a life and death struggle. They opposed any diversion of effort. This issue was discussed at a meeting of the Supreme War Council in Paris, presided over by the French Prime Minister, Clemanceau. Lloyd George pressed for diversion of divisions to the eastern theatre. Clemenceau asked Robertson for his professional advice. His advice was contrary to that of his Prime Minister. Lloyd George was furious. Soon after the meeting, he sacked Robertson. A few months later the Germans launched their big offensive of 1918 which the Allies beat back by the skin of their teeth. Things may have been very different had divisions been diverted from France. Lloyd George realised his mistake. He promoted Robertson, then living in retirement, to the rank of Field Marshal.

There were no major civil military differences in the Second World War. After that war, a big controversy arose between Truman and MacArthur. The issues involved were of global dimension. MacArthur was the greatest American military leader of all times. He had earned accolades in the First World War. He was the youngest Major General in France who flamboyantly led his division from the front in battles. He was called the bravest of the brave in a brave division. Truman was then serving as a Captain in France. MacArthur became Chief of the US Army and on retirement was Military Adviser in the Phillipines, when Japan attacked Pearl Harbour. He was recalled to colours. He blazed a trail of victories from Australia to Tokyo and took the surrender of Japan. After the war, he became a most successful Pro Consul in history, rehabilitating and resurrecting Japan. His military genius was again put to test during the Communist invasion of South Korea. His masterly strategic stroke of Inchon Landings saved South Korea. He undertook this hazardous operation against the advice of the American Chiefs of Staff. Well into his Seventies, he personally conducted the operation from a warship off the coast at Inchon. He now came to have differences with Truman. MacArthur wanted an all out offensive against the Communists. He said in Europe, Communism was being fought at conference tables while in Asia he was fighting it on the battlefield. He wanted a nuclear waste to be laid along the Yalu river against Chinese intervention in Korea and an all out offensive against China in Manchuria and from Formosa into the Chinese mainland. He warned that if China was not neutralised, Communism would spread in Asia. Prophetically, he added that Tibet and Indo-China (now Viet Nam, Laos and Cambodia), would suffer Communist rule. Truman wanted the war to be limited to Korea. Europe was still recovering from the ravages of the Second World War and the Allied Powers did not support MacAerhur's war plan. Moreover, the Soviet Union had now become a nuclear weapon power. This carried the risk of a nuclear conflagration. MacArthur made indiscreet remarks to the Press. He said that he did not know the aim of the war in Korea adding that in war there was no substitute to victory. He wrote a private letter to an American Senator expounding his strategic views, which the latter leaked to the Press. Truman promptly dismissed MacArthur unceremoniously. At his departure the Japanese in lakhs lined up the road to Tokyo airport to bid him farewell. He received an unprecedented ticker tape reception on arrival in New York. His brilliant address at the Amercan Congress saying old soldiers never die, they only fade away, swept the Nation. Yet it was realised that there could be no compromise with the supremacy of the civil. MacArthur was ill advised to voice contrary views whilst still in uniform. He should have resigned and then placed his views before the people to decide. However, the people's regard for MacArthur did not diminish. In a fitting recognition of his service to the Nation, he was summoned to a special session of the Congress at which a gold medal, struck in his honour, was presented to him. The medal had the following words inscribed on it – Pride of America, Saviour of Australia, Liberator of the Phillipines, Conqueror of Japan and Defender of Korea.

There have been hiccups in civil military relations in India. General Thimayya was a most charismatic leader. He was the only Indian to command a brigade in war during the British period. He personally led the attack in the battle of Zoji La in Kashmir. For the first time in history tanks of 7 cavalry had been used at that high altitude. As Chairman of the Neutral Nations Commission in Korea, he received international recognition. As Army Chief, his relations with Krishna Menon soured. He resigned over the promotion of a Major General to Lieutenant General. Nehru persuaded him to withdraw his resignation. This greatly damaged his reputation particularly when later Nehru criticized him in the Parliament. Had he chosen to resign on a more substantive issue like the neglect of defence of the Himalayas and stuck to his resignation, he would have gone out as a great hero and the debacle of 1962 would not have occured. The other instance was of rank insubordination to the Defence Minister by Admiral Vishnu Bhagwat over the appointment of his Deputy. He was sacked.

Obama's dismissal of General Stanley McChrystal is being compared with the recall of MacArthur. It is more in line with the dismissal of Vihnu Bhagwat. There were no policy differences. He was dismissed for insubordination and for clash of personalities. An article in a magazine, Rolling Stone quoted McChrystal and his staff using objectionable language for the President and his security establishment. The President was referred to as "disengaged and intimidated while dealing with the military brass". Contempt was shown for the Vice President. The National Security Adviser was called "a clown".

Special Envoy Holbrooke was described as a wounded animal and Ambassador Eikenberry was also criticized. Obama had no other option but to dismiss McChrystal. It is surprising that when he knew of the differences between these key officers last year, he had done nothing to intervene and sort out matters. General Patreaus replaced McChrystal. He was successful in Iraq from where US forces are being withdrawn. Afghanistan is a different ball game. Here US finances Pakistan and Pakistan finances the Taliban, who fight the US forces. This theatre of the absurd continues because US finds that it cannot fight in Afghanistan nor quit that country with honour, without the help of Pakistan. US appears to have abandoned its much proclaimed objective of liquidating Al Qaeda. The latter has been under the protective wings of Pakistan.

22

THE DRIFT IN LEADERSHIP

Ethics stands for moral values and is synonymous with morality. Public affairs stands primarily for politics which is the fountainhead of power in a democracy and it also includes other spheres of human endeavour like commerce, industry, administration, education and so on.

The city of Kolkata is of much later origin than our several ancient cities but it has played a leading role in shaping the destiny of modern India. Nineteenth century was a dark age of Indian history when Indians were not only groaning under foreign rule but were mired in ignorance, superstition, backwardness and deprivation. The survival of Indian civilization appeared to be at stake. It was then that the light of hope, reason, learning and knowledge shone from Kolkata to spread all over the country.

The past two centuries have seen three distinct eras - the era of the saints, the era of the Mahatma and the era of present day politicians. The era of the saints was when Swami Vivekanand and Sri Arbindo Ghosh from Kolkata preached spiritualism and humanism in modern language igniting a sense of pride among the people of India. Vivekanand's Chicago address carved a niche for Indian civilization and the Indian people in the world. Arbindo Ghosh with his fiery patriotism held out promise of a Great India. Apart from these spiritual leaders, Kolkata was the centre of intellectual activities with great social reformers like Rammohan Roy and Ishwar Chandra Vidtasagar, intellectual giants like Ram Gurudev Rabindranath Tagore, Sir Jagdish

Chandra Bose, Sir Jadunath Sarkar and great political leaders like Sir Surendra Nath Banerjee, CR Das and Netaji Subhas Chndra Bose. No wonder that it used toe be said that what Kolkata thinks today, the rest of India thinks tomorrow. The second era was the era of Mahatma Gandhi which showed how a suppressed nation on the basis of moral force can struggle successfully against the most powerful Empire known to history and attain its independence. This was a landmark event in the history of mankind. The third era is the current era of present day politicians when there has been complete debasement of all moral values not only in politics but in every sphere of life. Having lost its moorings, the Nation seems to be hurtling down towards an abyss, devoid of all values.

The Indian value system for a ruler was different from what obtained in the West. Unlike the West, where the monarch believed in the divine right to rule, the Indian concept was based on the theory of trusteeship. The concept of philosopher king was developed in Plato's Republic in 4th Century BC. only as a Utopian vision and as an ideal. Brihad Aryanaka Upanishad written three centuries earlier, talks of a ruler combining sovereign temporal powers with high intellectual attainments, one who performs the duties of a ruler with philosophic detachment, remaining above allurements of power and wealth, and following always the moral path. This was not merely a Utopian vision but was something actually practiced by rulers. Janak, Ram and Harischandra in the pre historic period upheld those values. Ashoka in the historic period was their worthy successor. HG Wells in his book Outline of World History has ranked Ashoka as the greatest ruler in the history of mankind. His Rock Edit No 13 states that the Emperor treats all his subjects irrespective of their creed, colour or caste as his own children. Our present day political leaders fall miserably short of those ideals for rulers.

During the freedom struggle when the Mahatma presided over the national scene and for the first few years thereafter, we had a galaxy of eminent political leaders. They were all people of impeccable integrity and character who had not only made great sacrifice for the Nation but were also men of great ability. Compared to those leaders, our present day political leaders look like pygmies, woefully lacking in all the qualities required of great leaders. Pursuit of power and personal aggrandizement are their sole motivating force. For the sake of winning elections they are ever too willing to sacrifice national interests and moral values. No doubt, India is now recognized the world over as an upcoming power of this century but the credit for this goes not to our present day leaders but to our human resource material. We won our Independence because of our political leaders. Today, the Nation has achieved success in various fields, in spite of our present day political leaders.

Let me now quote some episodes from the lives of our political leaders of the past to show the values they believed in. Mahatma Gandhi was the chairman of a school in South Africa. His son Hira Lal Gandhi had qualified to get a scholarship to go for higher studies in England. He chose the boy next below him for the scholarship. He gave his reason for this. Hira Lal's father could afford to send him for studies abroad but the father of the other boy could not afford to do so. At the height of the civil disobedience movement when success appeared round the corner, to the dismay of his followers he called off the movement because of the Chowri Chaura incident. Congressmen who had suffered atrocities at the hands of the Police gave up the code of non-violence and attacked a Police Station. Some Policemen in that building were burnt alive. The Mahatma insisted that both the end and the means had to be right. This demonstrated the superiority of morality over politics. The Mahatma was the architect of our freedom but when Independence came, he was not in Delhi to inaugurate our hard won freedom, leaving it to Jawaharlal Nehru to do so. He chose to be in Kolkata on 15 August 1947 trying to restore peace and alleviate the sufferings of victims of communal violence. Sardar Patel was chosen as leader of the Congress Parliamentary Party in 1946 by almost all the Provincial Congress Committees but the Mahatma chose Jawaharlal Nehru instead. The Sardar as a disciplined Congressman cheerfully accepted to be the Deputy Prime Minister to Nehru, The letter who was many years his junior. He did not leave the party and try to form his own party, as political leaders are prone to do nowadays. He served loyally as Deputy Prime Minister and achieved the astounding task of integrating over 500 Princely States with the Indian Union. His remarkable achievement was on a much grander scale than that of Bismarck who unified Germany. Princely rulers including the Nizam of Hyderabad, the richest man in the world of his time, had been at the Sardar's beck and call. Can there be a better example of financial integrity? Dr Rajendra Prasad, a brilliant alumni of Calcutta University who never stood second in his life, was President of India for eleven years. He was a true Gandhian who lived an austere life even in the splendor of Rashtrapati Bhavan. He drew only a quarter of his salary surrendering the remainder to the Government. On retirement he proceeded to live in Patna. He had not built a house of his own. He returned to live in the thatched house in Sadaqat Ashram from where he had conducted the freedom struggle in Bihar for thirty years. During the civil disobedience movement, Govind Ballabh Pant was leading a procession in Lucknow which was lathi charged by the Police. A lathi blow struck his neck and damaged a nerve as a result of which he used to be constantly shaking his head. In 1946 when he was the Chief Minister of UP, a case came up to him of an officer for promotion to Deputy Superintendent of Police. His staff told him that he was the one who had delivered the lathi blow on him. Pant ignored that, saying that the officer was doing his duty and carrying out orders. He approved his promotion. Lal Bahadur Shastri came from a poor family. He was married and had a child. He was appointed a paid worker of the Congress party on Rs 40 per month in 1920. He worked in Anand Bhavan at Allahabad. After a month, his wife told him that she was managing the household on Rs 30 per month and saving Rs 10. He took that saving from his wife and returned it to party funds. He got his salary reduced to Rs 30 per month. Later Lal Bahadur Shastri as Railway Minister, resigned owning moral responsibility for a rail derailment. Jaya Prakash Narayan was the hero of the Quit India movement and had worked closely with Jawaharlal Nehru in the socialist group within the Congress. After Sardar Patel's death, Nehru invited him to join the Cabinet as Deputy Prime Minister. JP declined the invitation. Had he accepted the offer, he would have become Prime Minister after Nehru. In the Sixties, JP was offered the appointment of President of India but he declined to accept it. The progenies of none of these leaders were allowed to take advantage of their lineage to get to the top in politics.

It is said that one evening the Greek Ambassador at the Mauryan court in Patliputra, visited Chanakya, the Prime Minister. Chanakya extinguished the oil lamp he was using and lit another. The Ambassador asked him his reason for doing so. Chanakya replied that the first lamp was his personal one which he used for his personal work and the latter was an official lamp which he used for official work. Lest this may sound a fairy tale, let me quote something from my personal experience. In 1948 I was a Major on the staff of General Cariappa. We returned from a tour of Kashmir and as we entered the General's house, we found that his other staff car had preceded us and his two small children with their school bags got out of that car. The General was furious at the misuse of staff car for private work. The ADC took care of the children as the General was a divorcee. He said that the children had missed the school bus. Therefore he had sent the staff car to fetch them. The General admonished him for what he called theft of Government petrol and asked me to take disciplinary against him. The next day the General asked me what action I had taken. I told him that I had issued a written warning to the ADC and he had expressed his deep regret assuring me that he would not commit such a mistake again. The General asked me about the loss of petrol to the State. I told him that we had taken care of that. Army rules permitted use of Government vehicles on payment of Rs 4 per mile and we had deposited Rs 24 for the six miles that the staff car had been used. The General directed me to make sure that the amount was debited to his private account. I have mentioned the incidents pertaining to Chanakya and Cariappa to bring out how scrupulous one needs to be to ensure that the resources of the State are not misused.

Today one finds that thousands of crores of public money are wasted in bringing out advertisements in newspapers to eulogise not only the Ministers but also the President of the ruling party. Such exercise in self-publicity and self glorification at the tax payer's expense never took place in the Nehruvian era. We are a parliamentary democracy in which the distinction between the Government and the ruling party has to be preserved. Khruschev as General Secretary of the Party and Bulganin as Prime Minister had come on a joint visit to India in the Fifties. Both were treated at par with the focus more on the former. We seem to have adopted the Communist style in which there is no distinction between the Government and the Party. In our case major Government projects have now begun to be inaugurated by the party President instead of Prime Minister or Minister. Terminal 3 of Indira Gandhi airport was inaugurated jointly by the Prime Minister and the party President with the Prime Minister virtually playing the second fiddle in mentioning this issue. I may be accused of being supercilious in raising this issue. I maintain that this is a core issue which cannot be ignored, if the culture of parliamentary democracy, as enjoined in our Constitution, is to be preserved.

Let us move on to other cancerous developments, which are destroying the fabric of public life in the country. The cult of dynasticism and the culture of sycophancy coupled with a permissive approach to corruption and crime, is totally destroying all values. We have unabashed dynasticism being openly practiced by most political parties. Generation after generation gets parachuted to the top position in the Government and the party. On the pretext of inducting young blood we have progenies of erstwhile courtiers brought into the circle of power, perpetuating a Mansabdari system. States have father and son duo serving as Chief Minister and Deputy Chief Minister. A Chief Minister forced to quit gets his uneducated wife straight from the kitchen who is not even fully literate and anoints her as Chief Minister.

Politicians are now indulging in gigantic corruption in a most blatant manner. The Bofors scandal was a chicken feed-fact compared to what is happening today. However, the massive cover up of Bofors case was a class by itself. Hardly any political leader booked for corruption has been convicted. The legal process keeps carrying on not for years but for decades. That reminds me of the remarks of Swift that law is like a spider's web which catches only the small insects, the big fish break through it. Elections are the root cause of corruption but no one wants to bell the cat and nothing is being done to amend electoral laws for rooting out corruption.

It is not only corruption but crime of every heinous type that has become rampant among the political community. This includes murder, rape, kidnapping, extortion and so on of course.

There are exceptions among politicians but alas they are very few. The Mahatma wanted political leaders to lead an austere life and the salary of a Minister limited to Rs 500 per month. Considering present inflation that could be made Rs 50,000 or Rs 1 lakh, but that is not enough for our Ministers. Recently two Ministers were found living in luxury suites of five star hotels paying lakhs a day. The Mahatma taught us that the end cannot justify the means. Both the end and the means have to be good. Today it seems political leaders work for wrong ends using wrong means. They have made a mockery of the Dharma Chakra in our national flag and of Satyamev Jaite in our national symbol.

I may appear unduly harsh on our political class but as I said earlier there are exceptions amongst them. Unfortunately, their number is very few. Holding the levers of power, our present day political leaders set the pace in the society. The Gita rightly says that whatsoever a high placed person does, the same is done by others. Whatever standard he sets the people follow. The poison from the top has now spread to all sections of our society. Corruption has become a way of life at all levels. Ethical values have been disappearing fast. Today we hear of teachers molesting children, senior police officers doing the same and committing murders, doctors trading in human organs, judges accepting bribes, army Generals arraigned for corruption, businessmen committing frauds and so on. The list is endless. On top of all this, we as a people are fast being swamped by consumerism and materialism, renouncing our value systems and our moral heritage.

I have painted a very dark scenario and offered no solutions. Frankly I am at a loss to suggest any solutions beyond quoting a Chinese proverb and repeating what the Mahatma taught us. The Chinese proverb is that do not curse the darkness, light a candle. The Mahatma advised us that if you want a change, be the change yourself. Let us all, follow this advice and individually do our bit. Let us spread the moral values and the teachings of Swami Vivekanand and Sri Arbindo Ghosh, all over the country.

23

COURTS MARTIAL

As a child I had an exposure to military law. My father was the Superintendent of Police of Patna and I was travelling with him by car to Danapur Cantonment, where a British battalion was located. The local Sub Inspector of Police stopped us and reported that a British soldier, Private Barney, had beaten a villager to death. His body was lying on the road and a crowd was assembling there. My father rushed to the spot. He ordered the body to be sent for post mortem and Barney to be arrested and taken to the Police Station. The Adjutant of the battalion with some British soldiers soon arrived at the Police Station. He wanted to take Barney away, for trial under military law. My father insisted that the soldier had to be tried under civil law as murder, culpable homicide not amounting to murder and rape, were beyond the jurisdiction of military law. The case was registered at Police Station and soldier handed over to the Adjutant for custody. This became a sensational case. Private Barney was tried in the High Court and convicted. This was my first introduction to military law and it stood me in good stead during my army career.

My first experience of a court martial was in Indonesia, as a Defending officer in 1946. I had to defend Aslam Khan and Mohammad Shareef of 4/8 Punjab Regiment. They had deserted with their weapons and had been taken prisoners, in battle, wearing the uniform of Captains in the Indonesian Army. At the summary of evidence, they had stated that they answered the call of Islam and were fighting for their

Indonesian Muslim brothers. They were charged for waging war against the King and for desertion with arms in war. Capital punishment is prescribed for both offences. I was at a loss as to how to defend them. When the summary of evidence was recorded they were not told that it was not incumbent on them to make any statement, but should they make one, it could be used as evidence against them in court martial. My request for a fresh summary of evidence, on this ground, was accepted. The accused now stated that an Indonesian girl had offered them cigarettes. They passed out on smoking these. When they recovered, they found themselves in an Indonesian Army camp. They joined the Indonesian Army so that they could get back to their regiment, at the first opportunity. They were convicted and sentenced to seven years rigorous imprisonment. They got away lightly considering that they could have been given a death sentence. They expressed their gratitude to me.

Pakistan invaded Kashmir in October 1947 but denied her complicity saying it was a freedom struggle that was raging in Kashmir. I had to collect evidence of Pakistan's involvement to be presented to the UN Commission due to visit India. I went to Yol, where Pakistani prisoners were kept. I met Aslam there. He told me that after Partition he and Shareef were released from Jhelum District Jail. They were hailed as heroes as they had fought for Islam in Indonesia. They were reinstated in the Army and promoted as Junior Commissioned Officers. He was prepared to depose before the UN Commission that he was with his battalion fighting in Kashmir. On return to Delhi, I learnt that Pakistan now accepted that her Army was fighting in Kashmir as the war in Kashmir was a threat.

I was associated with courts martial in all capacities except one. I have been a Defending Officer, a Prosecuting Officer, a member of the Court and a Presiding Officer. I have never been an accused in a court martial but in 1949 this prospect haunted me. All the civilian Dakotas of private airlines totaling fifty were requisitioned in October 1947 for airlift of troops to Srinagar. The enemy was approaching Srinagar. The situation was very critical. Working round the clock as General Staff Officer Operations, I was given the additional responsibility of organizing the airlift. Eight hundred sorties were flown from Delhi to Srinagar in fifteen days. This saved Srinagar. Commending this, Mountbatten wrote, "In my long experience of war, I have not come across such a massive airlift carried out at such short notice and so successfully". After the war, private airlines submitted their bills to the Government, running into a couple of hundred crores. It was found that there was no Government sanction for this airlift. There was also no record kept of the flights as I had not maintained any. Some people thought that I must have received a cut from the airlines. An inquiry was ordered. My bank account was checked but they found that it had been perpetually in red. I heaved a sigh of relief when a Government order was issued giving the President's approval for waiving all the irregularities and sanctioning payment of bills of all the airlines.

In 1978 I took over as Adjutant General of the Army and in that capacity had to deal with the courts martial of the Army at the highest level. I sent for the proceedings of the oldest available court martial and of the INA trials. The former was of Tantiya Tope in 1858. He was arraigned on two charges - waging war against the Queen and massacre of British civilians in Kanpur. Tantiya Tope asserted that he was in the service of his ruler, Nana Saheb and it was his duty to fight the British. He pleaded not guilty of massacre charge as he was neither aware of it nor present there. His involvement in the massacre was not established. The court pronounced him guilty of the first charge and not guilty of the massacre. He was sentenced to be blown from the mouth of a cannon. Bhullabhai Desai the leading lawyer of India defended the INA officers at their trial. Jawaharlal Nehru joined the defence panel. Desai's long address to the Court was brilliant. He did not argue that these officers had fought for a noble cause i.e. freedom of India. He concentrated on establishing that Azad Hind was a full fledged independent State as per international law. It had its own territory (Andamans Island), army, currency and postage stamps. The INA officers had to be treated as prisoners of war as per Geneva conventions and should have been released after cessation of hostilities. The Court convicted the INA officers but under tremendous popular pressure, the government was forced to release these officers. I ordered that the original copies of both these historical court martial proceedings be sent to the National Archives but their photo copies kept in the Record Room of Judge Advocate General.

24

WAR CRIMES IN BANGLADESH

The birth of India and Pakistan as sovereign States took place in the wake of a holocaust in which millions were killed and millions uprooted. Twenty-four years later, Bangladesh was born in the midst of extensive State sponsored genocide. Bangladesh maintains that three million people were killed and two lakh women raped. The Hamoodur Inquiry committee set up by Pakistan put the figure of casualties as low as 25,000. However, international sources have quoted casualty figures between 200,000 and three million. The Guinness Book of Records ranks the Bangladesh killings as one of the top five genocides of 20th century. The American Time magazine quoting a senior US official reported, "It is the most incredible calculated thing since the days of Nazis in Poland". Not long after Bangladesh came into being, founder of the State, Bangabandhu Sheikh Mujibur Rahman and his family were massacred in a military coup. Two of his daughters, Sheikh Hasina and her sister, happened to be abroad and thus got saved. In her first term as Prime Minister when Sheikh Hasina had a slender majority, she could not initiate action against the killers of her father and family. That process has now been completed. Recently, the death sentence on killers of Sheikh Mujib has been confirmed by Bangladesh Supreme Court. In her second tenure as Prime Minister, she has set in motion the process against the war criminals of 1971.

These developments take my memory back to 1971 when over 90,000 Pakistani soldiers surrendered to us. I was made overall in charge for looking after prisoners of war. Understandably, the common man in Bangladesh was seething with rage against Pakistani prisoners. We had to make special arrangements for their protection. Even some key civil officials in erstwhile East Pakistan including the Chief Secretary had to be kept in custody along with prisoners of war.

Our Government at the highest level decided that Pakistani prisoners of war should be treated in a most humane manner. Our aim was to send the prisoners back as ambassadors of durable peace on the sub-continent. At the same time, we had to ensure tight security for the prisoners, particularly the war criminals. Initially, a list of 400 war criminal was given to us by the Bangladesh Government. In July 1972, this number was reduced to 195.

It so happened that I had some previous experience of dealing with prisoners of war. In 1945 at the end of the Second World War, I was appointed Adjutant of the prisoner of war camp near Pegu in Burma (now Myanmar). There were 8,000 Japanese prisoners of war in that camp. This included some who were alleged to have committed war crimes. They were kept separately in improvised cells and the remainder had more freedom inside the fenced camp. Allied prisoners had been kept under abominable conditions by Japanese. Thousands of them died as a result of the brutal and barbaric treatment meted out to Allied prisoners working on the Siam railway. There was a desire for revenge among the Allies. All Japanese prisoners were required to salute Allied officers, irrespective of rank. Even though I was a Captain, Japanese Generals and Colonels had to salute me. They were given starvation scale of rations, below subsistence level. Prisoners doing manual duties were to be given higher scale of rations. I was not comfortable in treating the Japanese so harshly but there was nothing I could do about it. However, I tried to employ all the prisoners on manual duties for various work like road construction, repairs to ravaged buildings, camp duties, forest clearance and so on. This enabled them to get higher scale of rations. There was a reason for my having a soft corner for Japanese. At the turn of the twentieth century, Japanese had defeated Czarist Russia, then one of the leading powers of the world. The fact that an Asian nation had defeated a white colonial power, when Asia was under European thralldom, provided a fillip to our freedom struggle against the mighty British Empire. When I departed from the camp, Japanese presented an address to me saying that one day they hoped that I would visit Japan when they would be able to repay their gratitude. Till then, Mount Fuji Yama and the Sea of Japan will be anxiously awaiting my arrival !

We went all out to treat the Pakistani prisoners well. Considering how the USA treated Iraqi prisoners at Abu Ghraib and in Guantanamo Bay and what Pakistan did to our prisoners after Kargil, when they handed over their mutilated dead bodies, one needs to place on record how we treated the 90,000 Pakistani prisoners of war. They were given the same scale of rations as our own soldiers. We kept a record of their weight and almost all of them had put on weight while they were in our custody. More than half a dozen General officers were with us and they were accommodated in the Officers Mess at Jabalpur which was converted into a prisoner of war camp. Officers were given separate accommodation from men as required by Geneva Convention. We located prisoners of war camps at Bareilly, Agra, Meerut, Faizabad, Gaya, Ramgarh, Ranchi, Gwalior and Sagar. We took over the Central Jail in Agra and lodged the alleged war criminals there. Our combat units were deployed in forward areas and their empty barracks were utilized to accommodate the prisoners. When our troops returned to their cantonments, they stayed in tents for a few months, till the prisoners were repatriated. Facilities to play games like football, hockey, volley ball and basket ball were provided for the prisoners. There were recreation rooms in the camps for them with indoor games, reading material and radio. We had not then entered the television age in India. Cultural programmes like moshairas and film shows were held regularly. International Red Cross was allowed access to camps and when required, could meet prisoners individually. Both International Red Cross and our National Red Cross gave gifts to prisoners. International Red Cross transmitted their letters to their families.

I frequently visited camps and interacted with the prisoners. I met a few with whom I had served before Partition. Lt Gen AK Niazi, the Commander-in-Chief in East Pakistan was in

Jabalpur camp. He and I had served as Captains in Indonesia in 1946 and we knew each other. Muzaffar Hussain the Chief Secretary of East Pakistan had been a naval officer before Partition. He and I lived in the officer's mess on Wellesley Road (now Zakir Hussain Road) in Delhi before Partition. He opted for the civil service in Pakistan after Partition. There were a few other officer prisoners who had also served with me in the undivided Indian Army. We met each other cordially and talked about the old days. They told me that they had never in their wildest dreams could think that they would be treated so well by us.

During Eid and Bakrid, we used to organize Bara Khanas at which a goodwill message would be read out from the Army Chief. I remember participating in an Eid Bara Khana at Faizabad Prisoner of War Camp. A Baluch Subedar sat next to me. He had joined the Pakistan Army a year after Partition. He told me that in his over two decades of service, he was sitting with a General at dinner for the first time. He added that in his Army, Generals were too busy doing politics and that is why Pakistan had lost the 1971 war.

Our carefully planned strategy to win the hearts and minds of the prisoners had a good impact. Understandably, this did not diminish their desire to get back home to their families soon. Delay in repatriation worried them and some started getting agitated. They made quite a few attempts to escape from the camps and some succeeded. In a few cases, altercations took place between them and the guards. In two or three cases, the guards had to open fire in self defence. Such instances happened more in Agra where the war criminals had been lodged.

At the instance of UN, the International Red Cross organised a conference on application of human rights to warfare, at San Remo in Italy. Several countries sent their delegations to this conference. Pakistan did not do so. I led the Indian delegation at that conference. Geneva Convention to which India is a signatory, requires that as soon as possible after hostilities end, prisoners of war be repatriated to their home country. We had been holding Pakistani prisoners for over a year. The American delegate was highly critical of India fighting undeclared wars and violating human rights. He tried to make much of our holding on to the Pakistani prisoners for so long. I was asked to respond to his allegations. I gave a suitable reply contradicting his allegations. I spelt out in detail how the prisoners were being looked after by us. I added that a team of journalists from the US had visited the camp at Roorkee. They saw Pakistani prisoners and Indian officers playing cricket. They spent a whole day at the camp and interacted individually with a few prisoners with no Indian present. Los Angeles Times wrote that never in history have prisoners of war been treated as well as India has been doing. I explained that the prisoners had surrendered to the joint Indo-Bangladesh command. Pakistan had not yet recognized the Republic of Bangladesh and till they do so, Bangladesh was not prepared to repatriate the prisoners. Further, the case of the war criminals had to be tackled. The American delegate said that he had been informed wrongly and withdrew his allegation. India's stand was fully vindicated and there was all round appreciation at the Conference of the way we were looking after the prisoners.

A little before the Shimla accord, Sheikh Mujibur Rahman revised his stand on war criminals. He allowed them to be repatriated along with the other prisoners of war. He did this so that he could get Pakistan and other Islamic countries to recognize Bangladesh. The prisoners of war returned home as agreed upon by Indira Gandhi and Zulfikar Ali Bhutto at Shimla. On return, these prisoners gave a good account of how they had been treated in India. I was surprised to receive a personal letter from Nawaz Hussain, Cabinet Secretary of Pakistan, thanking me for treating the prisoners so well. Nawaz was in the Army before opting for civil service. He and I had served together as Captains in the Corps Headquarters in Indonesia. There were then only three or four Indian officers out of some seventy odd serving in that Headquarters. Nawaz and I had lived in the same office to mess for nearly one year and had been good friends.

Wounds inflicted by war criminals in Bangladesh were too deep to be forgotten. The people of Bangladesh have been observing Martyred Intellectual Day on December 14 when Pakistan Army before surrendering, massacred hundreds of Bengali intellectuals in Dhaka. During her second term as Prime Minister, Sheikh Hasina has opened the case of war criminals. Bangladesh has sought and received assistance from UN for investigating and prosecuting these cases of crime against humanity. UN has made four international war crimes experts available to assist Bangladesh. War crimes cannot be ignored and war criminals must be duly punished.

25

ASSAM ACCORD : BEFORE AND AFTER

Decades of neglect of Assam by Delhi and the unabated influx of illegal migrants from Bangladesh, encouraged by Congress for vote bank politics, had led to simmering discontent among the people of Assam for a long time. The discovery of 70,000 names of non-Indian citizens in the voters list of Mangaldai constituency in 1979 was the spark, which lit the fire engulfing the whole State. It marked the beginning of an unprecedented students movement led by All Assam Students Union (AASU) under Prafulla Kumar Mahanta. Simultaneously, an armed secessionist movement of ULFA (United Liberation Front of Assam) was launched from Sibsagar by Arbindo Rajkhowa and Paresh Barua. I had witnessed the Quit India movement of 1942. The students movement in Assam appeared more widespread with night black outs in cities, trains running empty, voter turn out a mere 3% in election on account of boycott call, and so on. After much violence and bloodshed, Assam Accord was signed between the Government of India and the AASU in 1985. It paved the way for a political party of students, Assam Gana Parishad (AGP) to come to power in the State with Mahanta as Chief Minister. The stand on illegal migration was diluted by accepting 25 March 1971 as the cut off date for identification of illegal migrants, allowing all those who had come earlier to become Indian citizens. The cut off date being demanded earlier was in the Fifties, when the National Citizens Register had been prepared. The Illegal

Migration Determination by Tribunal Act (IMDT) enacted in 1983 applied to Assam only with the rest of India covered by the Foreigner's Act. The onus of proof for citizenship in the case of IMDT Act lay with the State while in the case of Foreigner's Act, the individual concerned had to prove his claim for Indian citizenship. Besides, there were other provisions which made the IMDT Act a virtual facilitator of illegal migration.

Once in power, the AGP lost its focus on illegal migration. Apart from bad governance and corruption, it allowed the ULFA a free run of the State. After nearly five years the AGP Government was dismissed and President's rule imposed. The Army was brought in to deal with ULFA. Heavy attrition was effected on the ULFA. Leaders of the ULFA took shelter in Bangladesh and came under the patronage of intelligence agencies of Bangladesh and Pakistan. They did a volte face on influx of Bangladeshi illegal migrants. They now started targeting non-Assamese Indian population in Assam. The Congress Government of Hiteshwar Saikia continued with the Congress policy of encouraging illegal migration for building its vote bank.

The AGP came back to power in 1996 with Prafulla Kumar Mahanta as Chief Minister, but it did not have an absolute majority. It was now heading a coalition government. Relations between AGP and ULFA now nose dived and the two were in conflict. The ULFA targeted the convoy of Mahanta. He had a miraculous escape. In separate incidents, one Cabinet Minister got killed in an ambush and another seriously wounded. AASU continued to pursue the illegal migration issue but nothing tangible was happening beyond periodic meetings between representatives of AASU and the Government of India on implementation of Assam Accord.

I took over as Governor of Assam in 1997 and remained in that appointment for six years till 2003. Insurgency was at its peak in 1997 in the State. I had a long previous association with Assam during my army career and I was aware that illegal migration from Bangladesh was the root cause of insurgency in the State. I studied the problem in depth, carried out ground reconnaissance of the entire land and riverine Assam-Bangladesh border, interacted with political parties and discussed the issue with a few intellectuals in the State. The problem was over a century old. Its complexion changed from economic to political and then international. During the British days. Hardy peasants from Mymemsingh region of North Bengal (now Bangladesh), were brought to cut forests in Lower Assam and put the land under cultivation. Mullen the British Census Superintendent of Assam in the census report for 1931 drew attention to the changing demography of the State. He wrote, "It is sad but by no means improbable that in another thirty years, Sibsagar district will be the only part of Assam in which an Assamese will find himself at home". With the introduction of provincial autonomy this problem acquired a political dimension. On the pretext of Grow More Food campaign during the Second World War, Sir Mohammad Sadaulla's Muslim League Ministry in Assam started bringing in large number of Muslims from Mymensingh region for its vote bank. Lord Wavell in his book takeViceroy's Journal, wrote "under the slogan of Grow More Food what they are really after is Grow More Muslims". Afte Independence, Mymensingh region became part of a foreign country and this influx became an international problem. The Congress chose to encourage this influx to build its vote bank. BK Nehru, was Governor of Assam in the late Sixties. He took up this issue with Government of India but was told to ignore it. In his autobiography he laments that the old Congress gave primacy to national interests but now party interests are supreme. Ominous views coming from responsible leaders across the border could not be ignored. Zulfikar Ali Bhutto in his book Myths of Independence talked of Pakistan's claim to areas in Assam. Even Sheikh Mujibur Rahman in his book Eastern Pakistan, talked of land space for expansion and Assam being included in East Pakistan to make it financially and economically strong.

I submitted a 42 page printed report to President Narayanan with a copy to the then Prime Minister Gujral in 1998 saying that the serious demographic and security threats posed by illegal migration had not been suitably addressed by successive governments at the Centre and in the States. I made fifteen specific recommendations to deal with the problem, the most important being the scrapping of the IMDT Act. The other recommendations were, effective border fencing, floating border posts in Brahmaputra, registration of all boats, photo identity cards, updating of national register of citizens and so on. I also pointed out that it was not now practicable to deport millions of illegal migrants but they should be identified and made Stateless citizens with no voting rights or right to acquire immovable property. This would be in line with what had been unjustifiably done for the 30,000 Hindu and Sikh refugees from West Pakistan, who came to Jammu in 1947 and who with their progeny now numbered over one lakh. The other such refugees who came to different parts of India, got full citizenship rights. Two of them became Prime Ministers and one Deputy Prime Minister.

My report to the President was serialized and published in full in all the newspapers of Assam. It took the people of Assam by storm and they were happy that I had taken up this issue of great concern to them. However, on account of vote bank politics, the Congress party submitted a memorandum calling for my return.

Two of my recommendations were acted upon. Border fencing was realigned and the process of making it more effective begun. The previous effort which had been going on for Fourteen years, had been very unsatisfactory. I hope in the last fourteen years, the new fencing has reached completion. However, the State Government through an amendment to an existing State legislation has virtually brought back the IMDT Act. Struck dron by the supreme court there appears to be total lack of political will to tackle the problem in earnestness. However, I had the satisfaction to see some of the constructive provisions of Assam Accord implemented during my tenure as Governor of Assam. A state of the art oil refinery was inaugurated by the Prime Minister at Numaligarh. Two Central Universities, one each at Tezpur and Silchar were established. An IIT came up south of Brahmaputra in Guwahati. As Chairman of the Board of Governors, I was closely associated with this project and I saw it come up brick by brick. Professor Bargohain, the first Vice-Chancellor of this IIT, did stellar work in bringing up this fine institution, which is now a pride of Assam. The decision in Assam Accord to preserve the cultural identity of the Assamese people was implemented through putting up a fine cultural centre, Shankardev Kalashetra at Guwahati. At its inauguration by the President, I stated that India would now have three capitals – political capital at Delhi, commercial capital at Mumbai and cultural capital at Guwahati.

Alas, the problem of unabated influx of illegal migrants from Bangladesh continues unabated. This was the root cause for the Assam movement, which should have been resolved through Assam Accord. About one third of Assembly constituencies of Assam Assembly is dominated by Bangladeshis and so are eight districts of the State. We may well have a Bangladeshi Chief Minister in Assam. A number of Islamist organizations have now sprung up in Lower Assam. Yet it is still not too late for the problem to be tackled effectively if only we muster the required determination and political will to resolve the problem and usher Sonar Assom.

26

DIALOGUE WITH PAKISTAN

Much awaited July 2010 Indo-Pak dialogue ended in fiasco. Incidents of Cease Fire violation and bulk infiltration of militant in J and K during the days of hectic preparation and meeting in Islamabad, leave no doubt that Pakistan does not want peace with India before getting Kashmir on the platter. Military still rules there.

The origin and history of Pakistan has been of relentless hostility towards India. Jinnah, the architect of Pakistan had grandiose plans of reviving a new Mughal Empire in India. He not only wanted Pakistan to comprise the Muslim majority provinces in the West and East, but also a thousand mile corridor connecting the two wings, passing through well known Muslim cultural centres of Delhi, Lucknow and Patna. Besides, he put forward the legal argument that Princely States had entered into treaty with Britain, acknowledging the latter as the paramount power. After British withdrawal from India, those treaties would lapse and paramouncy should revert to the rulers of those States. They should decide the future of their State, in terms of opting for either India or Pakistan. Jinnah had his eyes on Hyderabad, hoping to secure largest princely State in the country, of the size of France. He even tried to lure the rulers of Jodhpur and Jaisalmer to join Pakistan! As for Kashmir, he was confident about geography and demography in favour of Pakistan. Kashmir would fall like a ripe plum in Pakistan's lap. The British were only too willing to oblige Jinnah. The Indian Independence Act of 1947, passed by British Parliament, catered for the provinces to be allocated to the two Dominions on the basis of religion and the Princely Sates on the basis of decision of their rulers. Maharaja Hari Singh's decision to accede to India was perfectly legal. It also had moral sanction with Sheikh Abdulla, the tallest political leader having maximum following in the State, endorsing it. Kashmir being a part of India is something totally unacceptable to Pakistan. They call Kashmir the core issue between India and Pakistan. Until the Kashmir issue is resolved, there can be no peace on the sub-continent. They have succeeded to an extent in putting this across to the international community, particularly the US. The fact is that this issue is not the disease but only its symptom. Even if it were to be resolved on Pakistan's terms, it would only whet Pakistan's appetite for bigger gains. In the context of international Jihad of Al Qaeda and other such terrorist organizations, Jihadi victory in Kashmir would be a step in the direction of establishing a Caliphate in the world. There is little realization of this in the international community.

Before Partition, Jinnah had thundered that he would have India divided or destroyed. His grandiose vision of a new Mughal Empire floundered. He could get only a moth eaten Pakistan. He now wanted India both divided and destroyed. Within weeks of Independence, he unleashed a tribal invasion under Pakistan Army leadership to annex Kashmir. Successive military invasions by Pakistan in 1947, 1965, 1971 and 1999 failed. From 1989 Pakistan has started cross border terrorism in Kashmir but that has been largely contained. Jihadi terrorism has spread to various cities in the rest of India. 26/11 was the mother of all terrorist attacks. Military which rules the roost in Pakistan under a façade of civilian rule, considers terrorist outfits as strategic assets. With increasing realization in the US, that the war in Afghanistan is not winnable and the US planning to exit with honour, Pakistan is now well placed to pursue its strategic goals in Afghanistan and at the same time continue targeting Kashmir and settle the issue on its own terms. For the last three years, Pakistan and its supporters in Kashmir have been trying to whip up mass movement in the Valley to break away from India. In 2008, it was the Amarnath controversy based on totally false and absurd propaganda. In

2009 the accidental drowning of two women in Shopian was projected as a case of rape and killing by the Security Forces being aroused against Security Forces at the death of some "innocent" stone pelting young boys. PDP a major mainstream political party has been hand in glove with the organisers of these three successive mass movements. It is significant that stone pelting operation with support from across the border was organized on the eve of the recent Indo-Pak talks at Islamabad.

Pakistan has a long history of violating written agreements. It violated the Standstill Agreement and invaded Kashmir in October 1947, the Cease Fire agreement and launched the 1965 war, the Shimla accord and started cross border terrorism and the Lahore declaration with Kargil intrusion. In 2004 Musharraf gave a commitment that Pakistan territory would not be allowed to be used for terrorist action against India but that continued unabated. Pakistan has always initially denied its hand in acts of aggression against India but subsequently the lie has got exposed by its own people and from overwhelming evidence. Major General Akbar Khan's book: Raiders Over Kashmir gave details of Pakistan Army's involvement in 1947 war, General Mohammad Musa's book: My Vision, showed how Pakistan launched the 1965 war, General Musharraf's book, In The Line of Fire throws light on Pakistani intrusion in Kargil. Pakistan's stand that there was no cross border terrorism in Kashmir but an ongoing freedom movement, was given the lie by a former ISI Chief Lt Gen Javed Ashraf Qazi in Pakistan National Assembly. Musharraf from Laedan has claimed pakistan's right to create trouble in Kashmir. In the case of 26/11, it has been the same story. Initially a denial that Kasab was a Pakistani citizen, then the Pakistan territory not being used for launching the terror attack and again perpetrators of the attack were non-State actors. Evidence by Kasab and Hedley has blown the lid but Pakistan is dragging its feet in taking action. On the eve of Indo-Pak talks, whether at the Foreign Secretary level early this year or the recent Ministerial level talks, hate campaign against India at public meetings and rallies were launched in a most vicious manner.

The story is no better in terms for observing civilised behaviour and diplomatic norms. Bhutto talked of thousand years war and referred to Swaran Singh as an Indian dog at the UN. Musharraf's breakfast Press conference at Agra violated democratic norms. On the eve of Foreign Secretary level talks, Qureshi in his speech at Multan stated that Pakistan was not on its knees asking for talks. It was India and that had done so. After the Foreign Secretary level talks Pakistan Foreign Secretary at his Press conference in Delhi made abrasive and objectionable statements at a Press conference in Delhi, ignoring diplomatic niceties. The recent barbs by Qureshi against Foreign Minister Krishna and India have been reprehensible.

India has always pursued a peaceful foreign policy. This can only be done from a position of military strength. Ashoka the Great had nearly a million strong standing army. We learnt a lesson in 1962 that peace cannot be pursued from a position of military weakness. Pakistan has been involved in nuclear black market and is the epicentre of international terrorism. It is both a rogue and a terrorist State. Libya for doing much less had been declared a terrorist State. No doubt India must ardently pursue the policy of peace with Pakistan but this must be done from a position of military strength and not under any external pressure. We should not be seen a soft State chasing illusions.

27

COMPARING BALUCHISTAN AND KASHMIR

The joint statement at Sharm al Sheikh mentioned Baluchistan. India is now committed to discuss Baluchistan with Pakistan. One needs to make a comparison between Baluchistan and Kashmir. Both have been in turmoil with ongoing militancy for decades. They are mountainous regions suited for guerilla warfare. Pakistan calls Kashmir the core issue. Kashmir is more a symptom than the disease. Baluchistan is the largest province of Pakistan with 43% of its land space and only 4% of its population. It is the richest province of Pakistan in mineral resources with gas, oil, uranium, thorium and largest copper deposits in the world. It is also Pakistan's most deprived province. All its people profess the same religion. Kashmir too is the State with the largest land mass in India but it has negligible mineral resources. It enjoys greater autonomy than all other States in India. It is the most pampered State with highest per capita central aid. As against India's national average of 26% below poverty line, Kashmir has only 3.7% in this category. Kashmir is a multi-religious State. Kashmiri Muslims are in a minority in Jammu Kashmir and Ladakh Insurgency in Kashmir is confined largely to Kashmiri Muslims.

The British signed a treaty with the Khan of Kalat in 1876 making Baluchistan parate but an allied State virtually like Nepal. Kashmir was a Princely State like several other States in the country. As per agreement signed at Delhi on 4 August

1947 between Mountbatten, Jinnah and the Khan of Kalat, Baluchistan was to revert to its 1876 status, on Pakistan becoming independent. Accordingly, the Khan declared his independence in August 1947. In January 1948 on a visit to Karachi, the then capital of Pakistan, the Khan was made to sign an instrument of accession to Pakistan. This was rejected by the State Assembly at Quetta and the tribal councils. A violent agitation was started by the brother of Khan. This has continued with varying intensity for the last over six decades. The Kashmir story is different. The Maharaja had not been able to make up his mind about which Dominion to join. Pakistan launched an invasion of tribal raiders led by officers of Pakistan Army. They were very near Srinagar on 26 October 1947. The Maharaja acceded to India. Sheikh Abdulla, endorsed this. The Indian Army flew into Kashmir the following day. It saved Srinagar and drove out enemy from the Valley. Sheikh Abdulla became Chief Minister of the State. After the first Indo-Pak war, peace prevailed in the State for over forty years. Democracy functioned and elections were held regularly. Having lost to India in three wars, Pakistan crafted a strategy of thousand cuts to bleed India. A low intensity conflict which is a vicious mix of insurgency, terrorism and proxy war is raging in Kashmir since 1989. The Valley was subjected to ethnic cleansing with over three lakh Kashmiri Pandits forced to flee. Militancy in Kashmir is fueled by religious fundamentalism. In the case of Baluchistan, it is assertion of a separate ethnic and political identity.

Pakistan Army has been conducting all out military offensive operations in Baluchistan, using air power and artillery. These weapons cause indiscriminate and heavy casualties. There has not been a single instance in which the Indian Army has used such weapons in Kashmir. General Tikka Khan, ruthlessly quelled the Baluch uprising in 1973. He was called the Butcher of Baluchistan. Musharraf was equally ruthless. He ordered air strike to kill Akbar Khan Bugti, the veteran Baluch leader.

Prompt action is taken in Kashmir against human rights violations. Pakistan Army Major raped a lady doctor in a hospital at Quetta. No action whatsoever was taken against him.

There are numerous proofs of Pakistan's involvement

in militancy in Kashmir, from thousands of Pakistanis apprehended there as also from documents and from international sources. Jihadis in Pakistan have openly declared war in Kashmir. A former Director of ISI as a Minister, during Musharraf's regime, admitted in Pakistan Parliament that the ISI had been organising cross border terrorism in Kashmir. On the other hand there is not a shred of evidence produced by Pakistan of any Indian involvement in Baluchistan. India has no geographical access to Baluchistan. She cannot do what Pakistan has been openly doing for all these years in Kashmir. Had India wanted to pay back Pakistan in its own coin, she could have done so in Gilgit Skardu region with which she has a common border. This region is legally Indian territory. For some time there was widespread unrest there.

Pakistan has raised the Baluchistan bogey to put pressure on India to withdraw her consulates at Kandahar and Herat as a first step to hustling out India from Afghanistan. Pakistan, the epi centre of terrorism in the world, is suffering at the hands of the Frankenstein monster of its own creation. She accuses India for terrorist attacks in its country even when its own terrorist outfits have been claiming responsibility. All this is being done to provide a fig leaf of justification for its terrorist attacks against India.

Index

C

D

Q

R

S

T

V

W

Y